The Medway Towns
river, docks and urban life

An England's Past for Everyone paperback

heritage lottery fund
LOTTERY FUNDED

INSTITUTE OF HISTORICAL RESEARCH

University of London
School of Advanced Study

VICTORIA COUNTY HISTORY

The Medway Towns
river, docks and urban life

SANDRA DUNSTER

Phillimore

First published 2013
A Victoria County History publication
Published by Phillimore & Co. Ltd, Andover, Hampshire SP10 2AA, England in
association with the Institute of Historical Research at the University of London.
www.phillimore.co.uk

ISBN 978-1-86077-728-8

British Library Cataloguing in Publication Data. A cataloguing record for this
book is available from the British Library.

Typeset in Humanist 521 and Minion

We wish particularly to thank the following VCH staff for their efforts during
the production of this volume:

Elizabeth Williamson – Executive Editor
Matthew Bristow – Research Manager
Jessica Davies – Publications Manager
Emma Bohan – Publications Manager (from August 2012)
Rebecca Read – Administration Officer

Printed and bound in Great Britain

Front cover: Ships laid up in the Medway, *c.*1675, artist unknown in the Dutch
    style. Image reproduced courtesy of National Maritime Museum.
Back cover: Phineas Pett, *c.*1612, artist unknown. Image reproduced courtesy
    of National Portrait Gallery.

Contents

Foreword

Strood, Rochester, Chatham and Gillingham were linked by Watling Street, the main road between London, Canterbury and Dover and the Continent where it crossed the river Medway. One can consider the Medway Towns in various ways. Rochester has a marvellous visual inheritance from the Middle Ages and later times, with its Cathedral, Castle and High Street. The early 12th-century tower keep, the tallest in England, dominates the town. Much of the cathedral is Norman and Early English. The public buildings in the High Street include the Guildhall of 1687 fronted with Tuscan columns and the Corn Exchange of 1706 with a brick facade and many 17th- and 18th-century shops and houses; in an adjoining road is Restoration House dating from Tudor and Stuart times, with unusual cut and moulded brick. Chatham was an ever growing dockyard where Nelson's Victory was built between 1759 and 1765. The town has a link with famous writers. Samuel Pepys in his celebrated diary of the 1660s records visits to Chatham when he was Clerk of the Acts in the Navy Office. John Dickens the father of Charles was in the Navy Pay Office at Chatham between 1816 and 1822 so that 'a very small queer boy' was to have happy memories of the town where a Jack Stronghill is thought to have inspired the creation of James Steerforth in David Copperfield. Strood with Rochester was noted for oyster fishing. Gillingham like Chatham grew from a village and like Chatham was the site of the dockyard and the houses of its workers. While histories have been written of each of these towns, this excellent book by Dr Sandra Dunster is needed to offer a single general history.

C.W. Chalklin

Preface

Between 1550 and 1914 the small cathedral city of Rochester and the three neighbouring villages of Strood, Rochester and Gillingham, all situated on the banks of the river Medway, grew and merged to form what we know today as the Medway Towns. Writing a history of the Medway Towns, each with its own distinctive character, was always going to be a challenge but thanks to the nature of the *England's Past for Everyone* project, of which this was a part, this was not a solitary endeavour. This book is the result of teamwork. Although I am named as the author, the business of researching, writing and producing this book has involved many people and organisations.

My greatest debt is to the team of volunteers from the Medway area. They contributed so much to the research for this book and their continuing enthusiasm for the history of their local area has been a constant source of inspiration. Working in groups or on individual projects the following people spent many hours working their way through archival material, transcribing endless documents, drafting material for inclusion in the book, or loading material onto the website: Andrew Ashbee, Gina Baines, John Basley, Odette Buchanan, Vikki Clayton, Catharina Clement, Margaret Crowhurst, Pam Doolin, Sandra Fowler, Sally-Ann Ironmonger, Brian Joyce, Peter Lyons, Chris Marchant, Rebecca Meade, Ben Morton, Astrid Salmon, Vic Salmon, Clare Scott, Roger Smoothy, Jean Stirk, Alan Watkins, David Webb, Pauline Weeds. I have acknowledged the particular contributions of individuals in the relevant endnotes. Not all of their work has made its way into the book but additional material, including transcriptions of probate material and census data for selected areas, is available on the VCH Explore website http://victoriacountyhistory.ac.uk/explore/.

I would also like to thank Robert Tucker for kindly allowing me access to his home, Restoration House, to photograph the decorative features that appear in Chapter 3 of this book. I am also very grateful for the assistance of the staff at Medway Archives and Local Studies Centre and the Centre for Kentish Studies who have helped me to track down material, scanned and photocopied documents and provided answers to my many questions about the sources with infinite patience.

Although the *England's Past for Everyone* project was financed by the Heritage Lottery Fund, without the University of Greenwich's considerable financial commitment this second EPE book on the Medway area would not have been commissioned. Thanks must also go to other organisations that have supported the endeavour financially: the Marc Fitch Fund, the City of Rochester Society, Kent Archaeological Society, Canterbury Historical Association, and Christchurch University, Canterbury. The latter offered the services of their Geography department and I am very grateful to John Hills for his map-making.

The Kent VCH Management Committee, Christopher Chalklin, Ian Coulson, Elizabeth Edwards, Andrew Hann, David Killingray and Peter Tann, have read and commented on drafts and offered advice and support throughout the period of the project. EPE and VCH staff have provided back-up throughout this project. The original EPE project team was disbanded in 2010 but they were a constant source of advice and encouragement in the early stages. Particular thanks must go to Professor John Beckett, who headed up this team and was a source of much needed constructive criticism on the first draft of the book. The VCH staff who guided me through the latter stages of editing and production are listed at the front of this book, and their help and expertise in bringing the project to a close has been invaluable.

Finally I would like to thank my husband George Whyte for his patient, sensible advice and diligent proof reading.

Sandra Dunster
University of Greenwich

The River Medway and the Medway Towns

This book tells the story of the changes that took place at the mouth of the river Medway in Kent from the mid-16th to the early 20th century. In 1550, the city of Rochester stood next to the medieval bridge across the river Medway and was strategically significant. Situated on the main road, midway between London and Dover, Rochester's Norman castle guarded the route to continental Europe. The small walled city dominated the local area, which included the nearby villages of Strood, Chatham and Gillingham. Over the next 350 years these four separate settlements would be transformed into the urban conurbation known today as the Medway Towns.

The motor for change was the river Medway, a waterway of local, regional and national significance. For those who lived on its banks, the river offered a means of earning a living through fishing, shipbuilding and supplying Chatham Dockyard and its ever-growing workforce. Its importance within the county was evident to William Lambarde who wrote in 1570 that of Kent's 'sundrie fresh rivers and pleasant streames' the Medway 'is more navigable than the rest, for which cause, and (for that it crosseth the shyyre almost in the midst) is the most beneficial also'. For the towns and villages of north Kent, the Medway was an important transport route for the movement of agricultural produce and industrial goods, promoting trading links with London, the east coast of England and with continental Europe.[1]

These local and regional advantages would probably have ensured the slow but steady growth of Rochester, Chatham Gillingham and Strood, but this book tells another and more dramatic story in which the area also gained national significance. From the middle of the 16th century the river Medway provided the nation with a strategically well-placed harbour which was close to the English Channel and the North Sea, only 26 miles from London by road and easily accessible from the capital by sea via the Thames estuary. Chatham Dockyard was home for the Royal Naval fleet from the 16th to the 18th century and remained an ideal location for building and refurbishing ships up until its closure in 1984.

The river Medway has dominated the economy of Rochester, Chatham, Gillingham and Strood. The business of building ships, and supplying and servicing the naval and military presence, overshadowed other industrial development in the area, at least until the second half of the 19th century. The river Medway was also an important route for trade and the transport of raw materials. Iron, timber, cloth, agricultural produce and fish left Kent via the port of Rochester, heading for London or continental markets. Although the cloth and iron industries of the Kentish Weald declined in the 17th and 18th centuries, the manufacture of paper, cement and bricks ensured the continuing wealth of the port of Rochester through the 19th and into the 20th century. The tidal river supported fisheries, and dairy produce was brought into the Medway Towns to be sold in the local markets. The position of Strood, Rochester and Chatham on the London to Dover road ensured a lively innkeeping trade to service travellers to Canterbury and to the continent via the Channel Ports. Tourists from London, only 26 miles away, also came to view the spectacle of Chatham Dockyard and ships on the Medway.

The legacy of the past is still very much in evidence in today's townscape. Buildings and open spaces which were once dockyard buildings, military barracks, forts and defences are now used for leisure, tourism, commerce or education. Industrial building such as breweries remain as a legacy of economic activity that was stimulated by or developed alongside the naval and military activity of the past. There are civic and public buildings which reflect municipal pride and the wealth generated by the people of the Medway Towns and the religious life of the area is evident in cathedral, churches, chapels and synagogue. The changing domestic environment can be seen in the few surviving houses from the 16th and 17th centuries and planned developments of the 18th and early 19th centuries. The terraced streets of the later 19th century, built to accommodate a rapidly expanding industrial workforce, are still in use today throughout Medway.

This book does not pretend to offer a comprehensive history of each of the four towns over four centuries. Instead it charts the development of Rochester, Chatham, Gillingham and Strood into a place which became known as the Medway Towns. It deals with the interrelationships between them, the dynamic interplay between their respective inhabitants, economies and politicians. The impact and presence of the growing naval and military establishments cannot be ignored but the spotlight here is on the local community. The book is structured in a way which allows the reader to look at the whole picture in chronological order, from 1550-1914. Alternatively each chapter stands alone, offering a snapshot of a particular period.

There are four interrelated themes running throughout the work: people, politics, the environment and the economy. The voices of the people of the Medway Towns – those who lived there and those who visited – provide a commentary on the place that they experienced. Historic images and photographs of historic buildings help to provide a flavour of the developing townscape. The political relationships between the towns, alliances and rivalries are explored through the records of local government. The dominance of the river and Chatham Dockyard in the local economy is evident in both local and national records.

The book confines itself to dealing with the period 1550-1914. The arrival of the English naval fleet and the building of the early dockyard at Chatham in the 16th century marks the beginning of the changes that brought about the transformation from a small city and three neighbouring villages to an urban conurbation. The book ends in the early years of the 20th century at a point when all four communities had achieved political parity and Chatham Dockyard had expanded to its fullest extent. The history of the Medway Towns in the 20th century is another story.

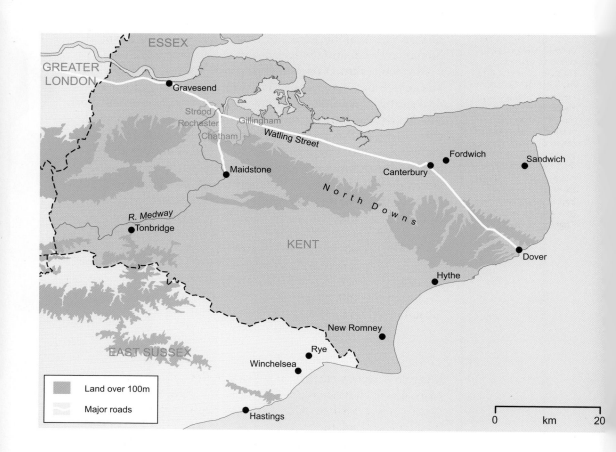

ESSEX

GREATER
LONDON

Gravesend

Strood
Rochester   Gillingham
Chatham   Watling Street

Maidstone   Canterbury   Fordwich   Sandwich

R. Medway   N o r t h   D o w n s
Tonbridge

KENT   Dover

Hythe

New Romney

EAST SUSSEX   Rye

Winchelsea

Hastings

Land over 100m

Major roads

0   km   20

Chapter 1

Arrival of the Dockyards, 1550-80

Figure 1 The position
of the Medway Towns
within the county of
Kent and in relation to
the Thames, Greater
London and the Cinque
Ports. Watling Street,
passing through the
Medway area, was the
main route from London
to Dover via Canterbury.
The river Medway flows
north-east across Kent
from its source just over
the county boundary
in West Sussex to the
English Channel.

In the first half of the 16th century the small cathedral city of Rochester dominated the mouth of the river Medway. Gillingham, Chatham and Strood were neighbouring parishes, reliant on fishing and farming. In June 1550, in the interests of national defence, the Privy Council decided that that 'all the Kinges shippes should be herborowed in Jillyingham Waters save those that be at Portsmouth'. This move was of national importance but it also marked the most significant turning point in the history of the local communities that sat at the mouth of the river Medway. The arrival of ships, sailors, naval administrators and shipbuilders in the mid-16th century was the first stage in the transformation of Rochester, Chatham, Gillingham and Strood and the consequences of these changes are still evident in the Medway Towns today.

So what was life like at the mouth of the Medway as the fleet arrived? Why were the ships moved to the Medway and how did the naval presence impact on local people? What was it that shaped the lives of the inhabitants of Rochester, Chatham, Gillingham and Strood in the mid-16th century?

THE LOCATION

The river Medway cuts a swathe through Kent, flowing 70 miles eastwards from its source in West Sussex to its wide-mouthed estuary in the north, making its way through every type of landscape and soil the county has to offer. From the clay and sand of the Weald, through the greensand soils of the Chart Hills and the chalk of the North Downs to the clay that dominates this section of the north Kent coast, the Medway finally broadens out to merge with the Thames estuary between the Isle of Sheppey and the Hoo Peninsular, fringed by marshland on all sides.[1]

It was on the narrow strips of marshy land on the riverbanks that the early settlements which would in time become the Medway Towns were established. Strood was to the north-west and Rochester to the south-east of a convenient crossing point on the river, positioned just before the river begins to widen into estuary. On the southern bank of the river, to the east of Rochester, lay the small villages of Chatham and Gillingham. Immediately behind each of these riverside communities were steep, wooded hills. The settlement pattern was typical of north Kent and the lower Medway valley with a dense network of tracks and minor roads linking small villages and scattered farmsteads.

There is evidence of Neolithic settlements in the area and later Rochester became the western administrative centre of the Celtic Cantiaci tribe. The Romans subsequently established a base on the riverbank at Rochester and built a bridge across the Medway. The importance of the location at the mouth of the Medway was further underlined when Augustine of Canterbury ordered the founding of a cathedral at Rochester in 604 A.D.

The place-names reflect both the ancient differences between them and the physical location in which they were found. The origin of the name Rochester is thought to be in the British name Durobrivis, meaning a walled town with bridges. The 'ham' in Chatham and Gillingham indicate that these were both villages or homesteads, the former by the wood and the latter the home of Gylla's people. The name Strood describes marshy land overgrown with brushwood.[2]

Rochester was about 26 miles from London and was on the main road between the capital and the port of Dover. In the 16th century, travellers from London along Watling Street approached the river Medway by coming down Strood Hill and through the village of Strood, which was clustered around the approach to the medieval bridge that led to Rochester. As they descended the hill, they could see the broad expanse of the river immediately ahead. Camden noted that the Medway 'foams and rolls with great violence and rapidity' as it passed under the 'magnificent stone bridge on arches'. Then as the water flowed into

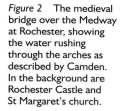

Figure 2   The medieval bridge over the Medway at Rochester, showing the water rushing through the arches as described by Camden. In the background are Rochester Castle and St Margaret's church.

the estuary the visitor saw, in the distance, that the Medway, 'now broader and gayer with its curling waves, washes most pleasant meadows till it divides at the isle of Shepy ... and empties itself into the mouth of the Thames'.[3]

Looking to the opposite bank of the river travellers saw the castle and cathedral towering over the walled city of Rochester, which, despite being 'in a very narrow situation', had spilled out beyond its walls with 'great suburbs to the west east and south'. Beyond this impressive but relatively compact urban landscape the heavily wooded countryside stretched uphill into the distance on the east and south and the river broadened out into the estuary to the north. Those who wished to travel further into east Kent, perhaps on to Canterbury or Dover, passed through Rochester's bustling town centre. Pausing for refreshments and perhaps a change of horses, travellers left the town through the Eastgate and crossed the marshland that separated Rochester from the village of Chatham. This small settlement was set among wheat and barley fields with sheep grazing on the riverside marshlands. The journey continued up the steep hill and onto the long, straight stretch of Watling Street, which cut through the fertile farmland that gave Kent its reputation as the garden of England. The village of Gillingham, lying on the riverbank to the north of the main road, might have been glimpsed across the fields, gathered around the church of St Mary Magdalene silhouetted against the sky.[4]

THE ARRIVAL OF THE FLEET

It was in this setting that the navy began to establish a base for the English fleet, close to the village of Chatham, at the point where the river turned to the north-east, not far from the boundary with the parish of Gillingham. The river Medway offered a safe haven on a deep and easily navigable waterway accessible from London by road and sea and which offered direct access to the North Sea.

Although the decision was made to move much of the fleet to the Medway in the summer of 1550, this was not the first time the river had been used by the English navy. During the reign of Henry VIII some ships were overwintered on the river and in the late 1540s considerable sums of money were spent by the navy on activities in the area. Records for 1547 show a wages bill of £4,167, but unfortunately do not state who was paid or what work was done. The same year a storehouse on the riverbank at 'Jillingham water' was rented for 13s. 4d. In the three years leading up to the decision to move most of the fleet to the Medway, riverside land and more storehouses were rented and £3,729 was spent on provisions for ships, known as 'victualling'.[5]

The decision to move most of England's ships to Medway in 1550 was made to meet national defence needs. England was on alert, fearing invasion. The threat the country faced had its roots in the 1530s when Henry VIII and parliament had rejected the authority of the pope over the church in England while France and Spain, the two most powerful nations in continental Europe, remained Roman Catholic. In 1538 the French and the Spanish agreed terms for peace, opening up the possibility of their joining forces against Protestant England. In the 1540s, in recognition of the potential threat of invasion, the south coast was lined with forts and the navy was strengthened. Ordering the fleet to the Medway in the summer of 1550 was another step in improving England's defensive position. Ships were near enough to the capital to be rallied swiftly in case of enemy attack and the move also eased overcrowding of naval vessels on the river Thames.

Overwintering, repairs and victualling were the main activities on the Medway throughout the 1550s and 1560s. Nine weeks after the original decision to move the majority of the fleet to the safe haven, the remainder of the out-of-service fleet was brought from Portsmouth with orders that the ships were to be 'calked and grounded'. In 1551 the navy bought a storehouse for 'victuals' in Rochester and the bill for provisions rose from around £3,000 in the 1550s to nearly £6,000 in 1567. As the volume of work grew, in

Figure 3 A map, c.1575-1610, showing, from east to west, the four communities of Strood, Rochester, Chatham and Gillingham positioned on the low-lying land between the river and the higher ground to the south. Ships lie on the river Medway between Rochester Bridge and St Mary's Creek (Saint Marikrike). To the north of this creek, the map shows 'West Marsh', an area that would become known as St Mary's Island. In the 19th century this marshland was drained for the expansion of Chatham Dockyard (see Figure 4).

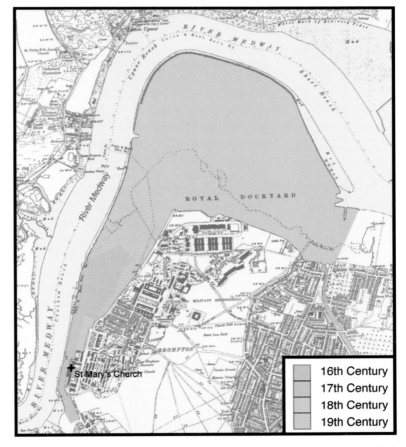

Figure 4 This map shows the phases of development of Chatham Dockyard from the 16th to the 19th century, showing the relatively small-scale development 1550-1600, modest additions in the 17th and 18th centuries and the expansion over St Mary's Island, which trebled the size of the yards, in the second half of the 19th century (see Ch. 8).

addition to the rental of storehouses, accommodation was provided for the officers overseeing the work. The accounts for 1567 record 'the rente of a house wherein the Officers of the Marine Causes doe mete and confere together of the weightie affairs of the said office *viz*. at Jillingham.'[6]

From 1567 references to 'Jillingham' ceased, and from this time forward the documents refer to the Medway anchorage as Chatham. There was also an increase in the pace of change and during the 1570s the yards expanded rapidly. A new mast pond, storehouses and a forge were built and at the end of the decade a new wharf was constructed and a crane installed to load and unload ships. In 1581 a graving dock was built for cleaning naval galleys.

All of this work required labour, both skilled and unskilled: 120 shipwrights and a substantial number of temporary labourers were employed. Most of the unskilled workforce was probably recruited from the local area, providing work for agricultural labourers in the winter months. Shipwrights were drawn from a broader catchment area. Although some local men would have had

the necessary skills from working in small private shipyards on the
Medway, to make up the shortfall shipwrights and other skilled
workers were brought in from shipyards and coastal communities all
around England. Skilled men who came to the Medway shipyards for
work were paid travelling expenses of one half-pence per mile for the
return journey to Chatham, as well as their wages.[7]

The spectacle that this activity produced on the river was worthy
of comment. When Lambarde wrote his *Perambulation of Kent*
he declared that the 'Harborow of the Navie Royal' was 'a thing of
all other the most worthie the first place, whether you respect the
richesse, beautie, or benefit of the same. No Towne, nor Citie, is there
… in this whole Shire, comparable in right value with this one fleete.'
Despite this patriotic admiration of the ships, Lambarde sounded a
note of caution, pointing out that the river had some drawbacks.

> As touching the harborow itselfe, I have heard some wish, that
> for the better expedition in time of service, Some part of this
> Navie might ride in some other haven, the rather because it is
> many times very long before a ship can be gotten out of this
> River into the Sea.

The difficulty of getting ships in and out of the estuary quickly was
a contributing factor in the decision to remove the fleet some two
hundred years later.[8]

ROCHESTER: A CATHEDRAL CITY

In 1550 there was only one Medway town. Of the four
communities, none but Rochester could claim urban status.
Despite the growing naval presence just along the riverbank,
the walled town with a cathedral, a castle and an ancient bridge
continued to dominate the Medway estuary for the next three
decades, both on land and on water, while Chatham, Gillingham
and Strood continued relatively unchanged as small village
communities at the centre of rural parishes.

In the 16th century, in addition to the small cathedral precinct,
Rochester comprised two parishes. The smaller, St Nicholas, was
entirely within the city walls and St Margaret's, the larger, covered a
small area around the South Gate within the city walls and a more
extensive area outside the walls stretching from the south side of
the London road outside the East Gate to the southernmost extent
of the city's jurisdiction (Figure 5).

John Speed's map of 1562 shows Rochester surrounded by a
wall on the north, east and south sides and bounded by the river
Medway on the west. Between the wall and the riverbank to the

Figure 5 The ancient parishes of Rochester, Chatham, Gillingham and Strood. The location of each parish church is indicated by +.

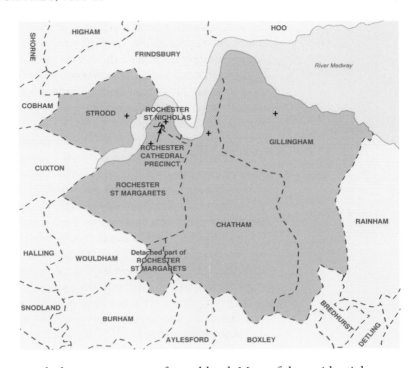

Figure 6 John Speed's map of Rochester 1562, shows the city from the west. Watling Street, the main London to Dover road, runs through the centre from west to east. The castle and the cathedral are to the south, bounded by the city wall. The main road, lined with residential properties, extends along the river. The open market place is on Watling Street near the Eastgate.

north there was an area of marshland. Most of the residential building was within the walls, although the map suggests that houses lined Watling Street for some distance beyond the East Gate and also shows buildings outside the walls to the south-west, on the riverbank below the castle. Within the walls the town was divided by the main road, part of Watling Street (now the High Street) that ran from the bridge in the west to the East Gate. The area to the south of the main road was dominated by the castle and the cathedral and the area to the north was more residential with houses and gardens. The eastern end of the main road was also the site of a large market place (see Figure 6).

Apart from the cathedral and the castle, there are few buildings still standing which were part of mid-16th-century Rochester. Satis House, on Boley Hill facing the castle and now part of the King's School, stands on the site of the home of Richard Watts, MP for Rochester 1563-72. Watts' house, clearly visible on a map of the early 18th century, was where the MP played host to Elizabeth I when she stayed in the town in 1573. According to Hasted, the Kentish historian, when Watts apologised for the smallness of his house, the queen replied 'Satis', implying that she found it good enough. Watts founded a charity which offered up to six poor travellers a room for one night and a gift of 4d. before they continued their journey along Watling Street. Although the Poor Travellers' House was almost completely rebuilt in the 17th century

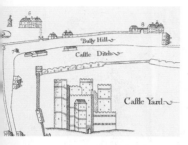

Figure 7 Satis House, home of Richard Watts, top right-hand corner of map, on Boley Hill, overlooking Rochester Castle (George Russell's map of 1717).

Figure 8 Richard Watts, MP for Rochester 1563-72, owner of Satis House and founder of the Poor Travellers' House and the Richard Watts charity.

and refaced in Portland stone in in the 18th, a rear wing still contains the original six small rooms.[9]

It is difficult to be sure about the size of Rochester's population in the 16th century, as the available evidence is somewhat contradictory. The number of taxpayers in the city in 1522 would indicate around 2,600 inhabitants while a government survey of Kent coastal communities in 1566, which counted 141 households in the town, suggests only between 700 and 1,000 people. It is likely that the figure was somewhere between these two extremes, around 1,500 or 1,600 in the 1550s. These estimates also confirm that Rochester was one of the smaller urban centres in Kent in the 16th century, outstripped by Canterbury and probably Maidstone, although Faversham was slightly smaller. Indeed, although Rochester is England's second oldest cathedral city, it was always overshadowed in Kent by Canterbury in terms of size and religious and economic importance. By the 1560s Canterbury had grown to over 3,000 inhabitants, about twice the size of Rochester.[10]

Although relatively small in population terms, 16th-century Rochester had all the characteristics that modern historians use to define the early modern town. It had a complex political structure, the economic activities of its occupants were varied and not predominantly agricultural, and its social, economic and political importance and influence reached beyond the city walls into the county of Kent.[11]

Rochester first gained its status as a borough through a Royal Charter granted in 1265. In 1465 a further charter stated that the corporate body was to be known as the Mayor and Citizens of the City of Rochester and this body was to be allowed to govern the city. The mayor and the 11 aldermen who formed the council of the City of Rochester were elected by the freemen of the city. Freemen had the right to trade within the city and were able to vote in local and national elections, returning two MPs for Rochester. The full status of freeman could be gained by birth, marriage, apprenticeship, purchase or as a gift of the corporation. Only a handful of other towns in 16th-century Kent enjoyed the privilege of borough status: Canterbury, Maidstone and the Kentish Cinque Ports of Hythe, Dover and Sandwich.[12]

Rochester was a centre for trade and commerce where markets were held each week on Wednesdays and Fridays. The twice-weekly market indicates the town's importance for local trade as most towns had only one market day. There were also twice-yearly, three-day fairs around St Dunstan's day in May and St Andrew's day in November. The market provided an opportunity for farmers from the surrounding area to dispose of any surplus foodstuffs and for local tradesmen to sell their wares. Apprenticeship records

Figure 9 The Poor Travellers' House on Rochester High Street, built to provide 'lodging, entertainment and fourpence each' for six travellers for one night. It was altered in the 17th century, and refaced in stone in the 18th century.

Figure 10 One of the rooms provided for the six poor travellers in the rear wing of the Poor Travellers' House.

show that trades carried out in the town included suppliers or processors of foodstuffs and drink, such as butchers, millers, bakers, brewers, innkeepers and fishermen. The processing of raw materials was carried out by curriers, cordwainers, tanners silversmiths and weavers. The clothing trades were represented by shoemakers, tailors and glovers, while barbers and apothecaries saw to the care of the body.[13]

The port of Rochester, which extended to include all wharves along the Medway between Hawkwood and Sheerness, was a centre for the transport and distribution of foodstuffs and goods by river to and from Maidstone, the Weald of Kent and London. London relied heavily on grain from Kent to feed its growing population. By the 1580s around 75 per cent of the capital's

grain imports came from Kent. Rochester, like other Kentish
ports, played an important role in this trade and most of the
wheat, oats and malt exported from the Rochester quays went
to London. A document detailing the cargo and destination of
ships leaving the North Kent coast from the autumn of 1552
through to the following spring shows that although the port of
Rochester lagged well behind Sandwich, Faversham and nearby
Milton in the quantities of grain shipped, three-quarters of that
grain went to London and the rest to other English coastal towns
(Figure 11). The importance of London as a market for goods
leaving Rochester continued to grow. The port book for Rochester
for 1565/6 records that, of the 40 goods vessels leaving the town
quays, 37 headed for London.[14]

Figure 11 Table showing
the destination and
quantity of grain exported
from Kent ports.

**Destination and quantity of grain exported from Kent Ports
1552/3 (quarters; a quarter = approx. 291 litres)**

	Calais	London	Other coastal towns	Total
Sandwich	1,485	1,867	1,306	4,658
Faversham	50	813	20	883
Milton*		976	236	1,212
Rochester		189	64	253

*Incomplete: details for October, November and February are missing.

Fishing was another important source of income for those living
on the banks of the Medway. In the mid-16th century catching
fish and dredging for oysters from the river operated under the
control of the Admiralty Court of the city of Rochester. This body,
said to have existed 'time out of mind', ruled over all the waters
of the Medway between Sheerness and Hawkwood and therefore
also regulated fishing and oyster-dredging from Strood, Chatham
and Gillingham. Courts were held twice a year, presided over
by the Admiral of the river, the mayor of Rochester. The right
to fish was reserved for those who were freemen of Rochester
and whose names were entered in the 'great black book' of the
Admiralty Court.[15]

The Admiralty Courts, held in Sheerness and Hawkwood
alternately, were an occasion for some celebration. The bill for
'vittels' for the gathering at Sheerness on 15 June 1569 came to
£2 2s. 8d. On the menu that day were boiled and roasted beef, veal,
a whole lamb, rabbits and gammon, bread and butter. The food was
seasoned with salt, pepper and vinegar and all was washed down
with beer and wine.[16]

A royal charter of 1460 granted the ownership of all fish and
oysters in the river Medway to the mayor and citizens of Rochester.

There was a wide variety of fish to be caught. The everyday catch, in season, was herring and oysters, but an early 17th-century charter mentioned whale, shark, porpoise, swordfish, lamprey, sturgeon, salmon and sole. These more exotic creatures, known as royal fish, were to be offered first to the Crown, then to the mayor and finally to the general populace.[17]

The survey of all ports on the Kent coast in 1566 suggests that although Rochester was home to the Admiralty Court, most of the fishing in the Medway estuary in the 16th century was done by a fishing fleet based at Gillingham. There were only six ships listed as sailing out of Rochester, of which four were more than ten tons, and the survey states that the 27 men who manned the vessels were occupied in both 'merchanndise and fishinge'. By contrast, there were 27 ships sailing out of Gillingham, of which 26 were small vessels of nine tons or less and only one a ship of 20 tons. All of the 43 men who worked these boats were said to be fishermen.[18]

Rochester's dominance of the estuary was also enhanced by its position at the point where the main London to Dover road crossed the river Medway over Rochester Bridge. Much of the road traffic from the capital into Kent and on to the continent passed through the town. This brought the great advantage of regular passing trade to the town's economy. Keeping this essential route over the bridge open and well maintained was in the interests of not only Rochester but also communities in the surrounding area and the Crown. The upkeep of the bridge was managed by two elected Bridgewardens, who from the early 16th century were from the local gentry. Repair and maintenance of each of the piers of the bridge was the responsibility of a specific landowner or parish in the local area.

Unfortunately, by the mid-16th century this system was failing. In 1557 Rochester Bridge was described as having fallen into 'great ruyne and decaye'. This was highlighted not only as a danger to travellers but also said to be 'to the utter decay of oure Citie of Rochester and annoyance of diuers other Cities townes and the parties thereunto adioyning'. A series of Royal Commissions was appointed to investigate the problem. By 1561 the bridge was deemed to be in danger of imminent collapse and a tax was levied throughout the county to raise the £2,000 needed for immediate repairs. Finally, a commission led by Lord Burghley and Sir Roger Manwood brought about the passing of the Rochester Bridge Act of 1576, 'An Acte for the perpetuall maintenance of Rochestre Bridge'. This introduced an annual election at Rochester Castle of two Bridgewardens and 12 assistants, a system strengthened by a further statute in 1585 which defined the electorate as two householders from every parish within seven miles of the

Figure 12 Rochester
castle from the south-
east. It was already
ruined when Pepys saw
it in the 17th century but
the mighty tower-keep
of Kentish ragstone
still stands 113ft high
and is one of the best
preserved Norman
keeps in England. It was
built *c.*1127 by William
of Corbeil, archbishop
of Canterbury, to guard
the London to Dover
road where it crossed
the river Medway. The
curtain wall around its
large bailey incorporates
walling from the previous
castle, built by the
bishop of Rochester in
the late 11th century,
and its semicircular
angle tower dates from
13th-century repairs.

bridge. This system endured until 1908, the wardens ensuring the
good repair of the bridge and managing of the income from the
bridge estates.[19]

Rochester Castle overlooks the bridge and by the 16th century was
used mainly as an armoury, storing weapons for use by the county
militia. The defensive importance of the castle and bridge in the
county was underlined by Sir Richard Sackville, speaking to justices
of the peace in Maidstone in 1561. He pointed out that the bridge
was crucial in 'the besyness of spedy transporting of ordenaunce shot
artillery and men for the defence of those in thys shere'.[20]

This would have struck a chord with the justices. Only seven
years earlier Sir Thomas Wyatt and his followers had used
Rochester Castle as a temporary base in their rebellion against the
Crown, prompted by Mary's decision to marry Phillip of Spain.
Travelling by road from Maidstone, Wyatt and his troops seized
guns from ships on the river and stayed overnight at the castle,
waiting to be joined by men from east Kent. Royal troops from
London deserted their commander the Duke of Norfolk at Strood,

crossing the bridge to join the rebels. Wyatt subsequently led his followers to defeat in London.[21]

Standing beside the castle, Rochester Cathedral was an imposing symbol of ecclesiastical presence in the city. Although the Dissolution had removed the monastic community, the smaller cathedral body which remained continued to wield authority and influence in and around the town in both ecclesiastical and secular matters. The new establishment was made up of the chapter – a dean and six canons – the ministers and choir, a school of two masters and 20 scholars. There were also six pauper almsmen and four servants.

The dean and canons were rarely local men but the people of Rochester did benefit from the presence of the cathedral chapter. The choir and the school provided opportunities for local boys. Eight choristers were given clothing and board and received training in music and catechism. Those boys who could read and write were offered a place in the cathedral school when their voices broke. The school gave five years' education in Latin to boys from poor backgrounds who were nominated to the school by the dean and canons. Boys who successfully completed their education at the cathedral school were then given preferential entry to Christ Church, Oxford.

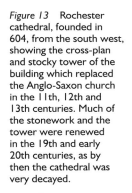

Figure 13 Rochester cathedral, founded in 604, from the south west, showing the cross-plan and stocky tower of the building which replaced the Anglo-Saxon church in the 11th, 12th and 13th centuries. Much of the stonework and the tower were renewed in the 19th and early 20th centuries, as by then the cathedral was very decayed.

The cathedral chapter was also a source of employment and charity for local people. The dean and chapter employed lay servants and were required to give £20 each year in alms to the poor of Rochester. This obligation was met and often exceeded, with an average of £28 being distributed each year between 1569 and 1613. The account books for 1550 show that 74 people received aid from this fund, ranging from clothing for poor children to help for a merchant who had lost his fortune at sea.[22]

The influence of the cathedral extended beyond Rochester's city walls. The dean and chapter were directly involved in the religious and secular life of north Kent as they had the right to appoint clergy in 22 parishes. Close links were established between the cathedral and the navy as the dean and chapter were also responsible for recommending clergy for Royal Navy ships at Chatham. There were also social and economic links between these two powerful organisations. In 1550 the receiver entertained a master of one of the king's ships and later in the century cathedral property was leased to naval officers and dockyard officials.[23]

THREE VILLAGES: GILLINGHAM, STROOD AND CHATHAM

The main settlements in Gillingham, Chatham and Strood were completely overshadowed by Rochester in the mid-16th century. Each was a small and relatively poor village in a rural parish bordering the river (Figure 3). The dean and chapter of Rochester Cathedral owned much of the land, with manorial holdings in each of the parishes at the end of the 16th century; the remainder was in private ownership. Today there is little visible evidence of the built environment of the 16th century. The parish churches, St Mary Magdalene in Gillingham, St Mary's in Chatham and St Nicholas in Strood, all stand on their medieval sites but all have been heavily rebuilt or restored since the 16th century. Few privately owned domestic buildings have survived either. One notable exception is Temple Manor, which lies in the middle of an industrial estate in Strood. It belonged to the manor of Strood, given to the Knights Templar by Henry II in the 12th century, and, as its core, still has a magnificent 13th-century hall house. In the 14th century it became a tenanted farmhouse and, after the Dissolution of the monasteries, both manor house and manorial lands passed into the possession of Lord Cobham. It was much altered about that time, with a new brick chimney to heat the hall and fashionable brick extensions either end.[24]

Most of the people who lived in these communities made a living by fishing and farming. Compared with Rochester, the surviving documentary evidence about Gillingham, Chatham and

Figure 14 The manor house and farm buildings of Temple Manor, Strood, depicted in the 18th century. The 13th-century hall-house, built by the Knights Templar to give hospitality to dignitaries travelling along the London to Dover road, is completely concealed by the brick alterations made in the 17th century. The manor had been a farm since the 14th century.

Strood in the mid-16th century is sparse but some of the parish records have survived and offer small details of everyday life. The population of Gillingham is estimated to have been around 300 in the 1550s. A comparison of the number of christenings recorded in the parish registers for Gillingham, Chatham and Strood suggests that the three parishes were probably similar in size until the 1590s, when Chatham experienced a rise in the number of baptisms, suggesting an increase in the resident population.[25]

The early parish registers for Chatham provide some detail about how local people made a living as the occupation of fathers was recorded in the first few years of the register of baptisms. This confirms that men in Chatham worked either on the land as agricultural labourers or smallholders, or on the river fishing, on board a ship or in the shipyards. For example, the record for 1570 shows that three labourers, four husbandmen and a yeoman, a shipwright, a waterman, and the 'cook of the Bull' all became fathers that year. The *Bull* was still in the vicinity a couple of years later when St Mary's saw the christening of William, son of Thomas Burnam 'bosun too the shype called ye bull'. The first entry in the marriage register for Chatham in 1568, records the wedding of 'George Mathew cooke to the Queens storehowse and Johne Smythe daughter to Nathaniel Smith, husbandman', suggesting that there was no great divide between the those employed in the service of the queen and those working the land.[26]

The parish of Strood flanked Watling Street on the western bank of the river Medway. The main settlement within the parish was clustered around the approach to Rochester Bridge. Its location guaranteed that it was affected by the passing traffic on road and river. In the case of the events surrounding Wyatt's rebellion, Strood was used as a base for the Duke of Norfolk's troops. According to a contemporary account: 'The Duke went to Stroud to see the planting of the ordnance. Which being ready charged and bent upon the town of Rochester ... the Duke commanded one of the pieces to be fired for shot into Rochester.'[27]

The church bell-ringers of Strood profited from the proximity of their church to Watling Street as they were often paid a few extra pence by the church wardens to ring a peal as royalty or eminent churchmen passed through on their way to or from London. In 1556, according to payments recorded in the parish records, Queen Mary, her husband Philip of Spain and Cardinal Pole all enjoyed this honour on separate occasions.[28]

In the mid-16th century the balance of power in the Medway area was firmly weighted in favour of Rochester. The ancient traditions of castle, cathedral, bridge and corporation ensured that this small walled city dominated not only the skyline but the politics and the economy of the estuary. Yet a process of change had begun. From the 1550s national government identified a new role for the river Medway as a home to the English naval fleet. Ships were brought onto the river for refitting and overwintering and a small naval presence was established onshore. From the 1580s the pace of change increased and the shoreline at Chatham was transformed. Chatham Dockyard, no longer merely repairing and providing a safe haven for the fleet, became a yard that also had the facilities to build ships. By the end of the 16th century the ships on the river Medway were accompanied by a naval administration which had put down roots on shore, setting up storehouses and victualling and ordnance yards, building docks and renting property for officers to live and work in. Chatham was to become home to the first English dockyard to offer the range of facilities necessary to support a fully functioning naval base.[29]

Chapter 2

A Home for the Fleet, 1580-1640

From the 1580s the Medway estuary and the communities on its banks became increasingly busy. Chatham Dockyard, which for the previous thirty years had offered a safe harbour for the fleet, now became a site for the preparation of the English fleet for war. There were two periods of intense activity in the dockyard. The first was during the preparations to fight the Spanish Armada in the 1580s and the second some thirty years later when England was at risk of war with the Dutch. International conflict was the driving force behind the expansion of Chatham Dockyard, an increase in the local population and changes in the built environment of the Medway Towns.

THE 1580S: DEFENCE AGAINST THE ARMADA

The marriage of Mary Tudor and Philip II had safeguarded an Anglo-Spanish alliance, but following Mary's death the relationship between the two countries worsened steadily over the next thirty

Figure 15 A map of the Medway, c.1590, showing defensive beacons in Upnor to the north and Chatham to the south, Upnor Castle to the west and a ship guarding the chain across the Medway between the castle and St Mary's Creek. Upnor Castle (see Figure 38) was an artillery fort built overlooking the Medway to protect warships at Chatham. Built in 1559, the fort was remodelled between 1559-1601.

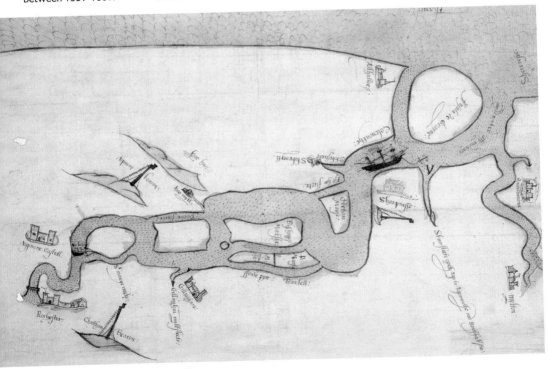

Figure 16 An English pinnace, a small two-masted ship, fighting the Spanish Armada.

years. When Elizabeth I took the throne in 1558 she refused to marry either her sister's widower or his cousin Archduke Charles and her rejection of the Roman Catholic faith put a further distance between the two nations. Diplomatic relations declined further in the 1570s and '80s as England backed the Netherlands in their revolt against Spanish rule, the English raided Spanish treasure ships in the New World and Elizabeth sanctioned the execution of the Catholic Mary Queen of Scots. Philip I of Spain ordered the preparation of the Armada in 1586. The Spanish plan was to send their fleet to secure a landing on the Kent coast and then to ferry an invading army across from the Netherlands.

As fears of a Spanish invasion grew, defences at Chatham Dockyard were improved. In 1580 St Mary's Creek, to the north of the yards, was blocked with stakes to stop enemy ships using it to avoid the guns at Upnor Castle, and a chain which could be raised and lowered was placed across the river between Upnor and St Mary's Creek. The installation of the chain was 'tedyous and cumbersome' and cost £610 but by 1585 it was in place, guarded by two small ships at either end. Watchmen were stationed onshore and ships patrolled the coastline to offer advance warning of the approach of enemy ships. Beacons were set along the Kent coast, including one at Chatham and another at Upnor. They were to be lit as a signal of invasion and as a call to all men aged 16-60 to gather to defend the shore. In 1586, as tension mounted, additional ships were lit up at night and moored on the outer reaches of the Medway estuary to watch for an invasion and carry the news swiftly upriver to Upnor and Rochester.[1]

At the same time the fleet was prepared for action. Under the supervision of Matthew Baker, the first Master Shipwright and Principal Officer of the dockyards at Chatham, ships were overhauled and readied for battle. 1586 saw the completion of

Figure 17 Graph showing the number of riggers and crew employed at Chatham from June 1587 to January 1588 in preparation for the Armada.[2]

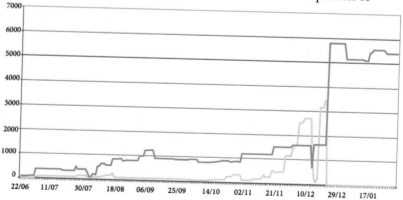

— riggers — crew

Figure 18 English ships defeating the Spanish Armada, August 1588. The English vessels fly the flag of St George with a red cross on a white background and the Spanish vessels a yellow cross on a red background.

the *Sunne*, the first ship known to have been built at Chatham. £150 was paid 'for a newe pinnace by him made for her highness at Chatham named the Sunne of 48 foote in length and 13 foot in breadth'. This small, two-masted vessel sailed with the Armada fleet with a crew of 26 and four gunners, under the command of Richard Buckley.[3]

The scale of the operation to prepare the fleet for battle was enormous, with increasing numbers of riggers and crew employed at Chatham between June 1587 and January 1588 (Figure 17). In the final weeks of preparation there were over 3,000 men working to rig the ships and more than 5,000 hired as crew. It is difficult to imagine the impact that the influx of this many people had on the residents of Chatham and the surrounding area. The rapidly expanding population had to be housed, fed and watered. While seamen and some workmen would have been berthed on their ships, a letter of 1595 suggests that local people took the opportunity to profit from the peaks of demand for labour by offering board and lodging to the incoming workforce.

> George Westill of Chatham Labourer (a poore man that serveth her Majestie in the woorke heare, as a labourer) havinge in his house 4 spare bedds fytt to lodge Artificers as neede requireth, did (about a yeare past) take into his house ... to lodge and boorde 8 Shipwrights, and Calkers, that then served in her Majesties woorkes heare, suche as weare called to service from London, and other partes of the Realme.[4]

Shipbuilding in the 16th century

Building a ship in the 16th century was a labour-intensive activity involving a labour force of around 140 men, including joiners, carpenters, riggers, caulkers, sail-makers and labourers. The work was overseen by a master shipwright who was responsible for the design and construction of the ship, the day-to-day running of the dockyard and for buying in supplies and raw materials.

Ships were built from wood, which needed to be well seasoned to ensure the planks would not shrink or split in the water. English oak was used for the hull as it is strong and water-resistant but other woods such as elm and beech were also used in fitting out the ship, while fir or pine was suitable for the masts.

Shipbuilding for the royal fleet in the second half of the 16th century was mainly done at Deptford and Woolwich, conveniently located on the Thames, close to London and to good supplies of wood in the forests of Kent and Sussex. The work was overseen by royally appointed master shipwrights from the Pett and Baker families.

Figure A *An illustration from Matthew Baker's* Fragments of Ancient Shipwrightry *(1586) showing the narrowing of the hull of a galleon, which is thought to have contributed to the speed of the English fleet when fighting the Spanish Armada.*

Matthew Baker (1530-1613)

A significant innovation to the art of the shipwright, introduced by Baker, was the practice of creating drawings for the plan of a ship, rather than working from a scale model or 'laying down the lines' in the shipbuilding yard. His book, *Fragments of Ancient Shipwrightry* (1586), is the earliest surviving English work on shipbuilding.

Early shipbuilding at Chatham

In 1571 Matthew Baker was appointed Master Shipwright at Chatham. Initially his work was to direct the routine maintenance of the royal fleet stationed on the Medway and to survey the condition of the ships. It was under Baker's rule that the first ships were built at Chatham. The first, the *Sunne*, was a 56-ton pinnace, a small three-masted vessel of a kind originally designed as a trading ship but often used as a tender to warships. The second was the *Seven Stars*, a galleon of 140 tons. Both were launched in 1586. Chatham did not come into its own as a shipbuilding yard until a dry dock was built there in the early 17th century.

Figure 19 Lord Howard, Lord High Admiral and commander-in-chief of the navy at the time of the Armada.

Figure 20 Sir John Hawkins (1532-95) was one of the leading seamen of the 16th century, knighted for his role in the Armada. He was founder of the Chatham Chest and the Sir John Hawkins Hospital in Chatham.

By the end of 1587 the ships were prepared for battle and Lord Howard, the newly appointed commander-in-chief of the fleet, went to Medway to inspect the vessels that had gathered there. He was satisfied with what he found, declaring that 'There is not one but I durst go to the Rio del Plata in her.' The ships sailed from Chatham on 29 April 1588, heading for Plymouth, where they joined the rest of the fleet, commanded by Sir Francis Drake, and went on to defeat the Spanish.

After the battle was won, many of the sailors who returned to Kent were wounded or sick and many died. Howard reported from the east Kent coast that:

> Sickness and mortallitie begin wonderfullie to grow amongst us: and yt is a most pitifulle sighte to see here at Margate, how the men, having no place to receive them into here, dye in the streets … It would grieve anie man's harte so to see theme that have served so valiantlie to dye so miserabillie.

This suffering is said to have prompted Sir John Hawkins and Sir Francis Drake to set up a national scheme which aimed to provide for the 'perpetual relief of such mariners, shipwrights, and seafaring men' who were unable to work 'by reason of hurts and maims received in the service'. The charity, named the Chatham Chest after the sturdy coffer in which the funds were kept, was funded by serving seamen contributing five per cent of their monthly salary of 10s. Despite the precaution of the chest having five locks and five keyholders, the management of the fund was questionable, with the administrators often receiving greater benefit than the seamen, and by 1660 the Chest was in debt. The charity never fully recovered its management and was transferred to the naval hospital at Greenwich in 1803. Hawkins also set up a 'hospital' for elderly seamen and shipwrights from Chatham, giving 12 men their own room and two shillings a week. The charity was endowed with land to support it and survives to this day.[5]

Following the defeat of the Armada, Chatham remained the leading English dockyard. More government money was spent at Chatham than at Portsmouth, Woolwich and Deptford combined. For example, in 1606 £1,842 was spent on Chatham and only £60 on the other three yards.[6]

Chatham enjoyed several local advantages. It had easy access to the natural resources and manufactured goods of the Weald of Kent. At the beginning of the 17th century, this part of the county offered a plentiful supply of the timber needed for shipbuilding. The Wealden iron industry manufactured nails, guns and cannon in foundries in the area around Tonbridge and

Figure 21 Sir John
Hawkins Hospital,
founded in 1594 for poor
seamen, shipwrights and
their wives. The two
rows of small houses
flanking a central Council
room were built in
1789-90 to replace the
original almshouses.
In the 19th century
another row was added
behind the Council
room, on a plot that
stretches from Chatham
High Street almost to
the river. The houses
have been converted
to eight flats, all still
intended for seamen or
related personnel.

all of these essential goods could be easily transported downriver to the estuary.[7]

Other reasons for the continuing popularity of Chatham as the main English naval base were noted by Sir William Monson early in the 17th century. In Monson's opinion, the anchorage on the Medway was secure and offered 'sufficient space for every ship to ride without annoying one another'. Repairs and maintenance were easily carried out because 'The water at Chatham flows sufficiently every spring tide to grave the greatest ships'. Naval officers and their families were already established in the area and the proximity of the Medway to London and the Thames offered advantages, ensuring the navy could be 'supplied with all things they shall stand in need of, for that London is the storehouse of all England … no part of England can victual a navy so conveniently, speedily and at so small a charge as London'. The port of London was a good source of seamen and the Thames dockyards could provide skilled labour for work in the Medway yards and additional facilities in a crisis.

Monson also acknowledged Chatham's drawbacks. He observed that the river was difficult to navigate and pointed out, with some foresight, that if England went to war with the Netherlands the anchorage was 'not altogether so safe and secure from the assault of a fleet that shall be brought with an easterly wind'. Despite this he concluded that 'Chatham is the best and safest place, and I wish that our whole navy may be kept at Chatham'. Admiral Monson was not alone in his support for the location and in 1618-26 a new period of expansion began in Chatham Dockyard.[8]

The responsibility for improvements was given to Phineas Pett, an ambitious master shipwright from a well-established shipbuilding family. He had first been employed at Chatham as Keeper of the Stores in 1600 and became a Master Shipwright in 1604. By 1608 he was at the centre of a fraud investigation, accused of a variety of scams, including using naval supplies for private shipbuilding, overcharging for repairs and pocketing the difference, and taking a cut of the profits made from the over-supply of stores. Despite the weight of evidence against him, he escaped punishment. According to Pett himself, King James was 'sufficiently persuaded of my honesty, integrity and abilities'. In 1630 Pett became the first resident Commissioner of Chatham Dockyard, giving him overall responsibility for the running of the yard and the privilege of a seat on the Navy Board in London. He remained in post at Chatham until his death in 1647.[9]

The expansion of the yard required new land. An additional 80 acres was leased: nine from the dean and chapter of Rochester cathedral and 71 from Sir Robert Jackson, 'part whereof is used for the newe dockyard and ropeway part for a brycke and lyme kilne and part for waies to the Dockes and kylnes'. New dry docks, a graving dock and a mast dock, a sail loft and a rope house and residences for the naval officers were created in 1619-26. At the same time there were references to the rent of a house 'for laying upp of provisions', and £1 paid for the rent of 'certaine grounds whereon storehouses are builded'.[10]

A significant building in the landscape of Chatham Dockyard at this time was Hill House (also referred to as Queen's House), described in 1570 as 'a house wherein the Officers of the Marine Causes doe mete and confere together of the weightie affairs of the said office'. In the 1580s Peter Pett, master shipwright, was lodged there. His son Phineas recorded that as a child he 'lay in my father's lodgings in the Queen's House from Whence I went every day to school to Rochester and came home at night for three years space'. Samuel Pepys visited in 1661, referring to it as 'a pretty, pleasant house'. The house was used by the Admiralty until the mid-18th century and demolished in the early 19th century to make way for the Royal Marine Barracks.[11]

Expansion brought changes in the yard and in the workforce. Although repairs and improvements to the naval fleet continued, from the 1620s the main purpose of the yard was to build new ships. This required a large skilled workforce. By the 1620s there were around 250 people employed in the yard. At this stage it was still necessary to bring skilled workers to the area. Shipwrights, mast makers, caulkers, joiners and sail makers, recruited from other shipyards around the country, were offered a lodgings allowance and travelling money on top of wages of around 2s. per week. Unskilled workers were recruited from the local villages,

Figure 22 Portrait of Phineas Pett, Master Shipwright, appointed first resident Commissioner of Chatham Dockyard in 1630.

Figure 23 Hill House, Chatham Dockyard, used by the Admiralty as a meeting place and lodging house for officers from the 16th to the 18th century.

attracted to the docks by the opportunity to supplement income from smallholdings or agricultural labour.

Shipbuilding on this scale created an unusually large concentration of labour in one place for the 17th century, turning the banks of the Medway into an industrial site. Both skilled and unskilled worked long hours, from dawn until dusk, and the work was divided into discrete specialist tasks. But this was not the regimented industry of the 19th century. The pace of work was often slow and at times erratic. Dockyard workers did not necessarily come to work every day and the yards were open to all. Families and visitors came and went as they pleased throughout the working day.[12]

The crisis of the 1590s

The decade after the defeat of the Armada was a tense period in the Medway Towns. The threat of a Spanish invasion still loomed, keeping local militia on alert. There were food shortages and disease throughout England and Kent did not escape this problem. From 1593-5 the county was visited by plague, and outbreaks of smallpox and influenza also took their toll. Chatham landlord George Westill lost his income from renting out rooms to dockyard workers for several months in 1595 when 'the pestelence happened into the same house, whereuppon his doores weare shutt upp, and so less lodginge till about the first of Julye last att what tyme the house beinge purged from the infeccion, he tooke againe 8 calkers, and carpenters, to lodge'. The parish registers of burials for Chatham show an increase of one third over the previous decade. In Gillingham the increase was even more marked, with nearly twice as many people dying in the 1590s as in the 1580s.[13]

From 1594-7 summer frosts and heavy rain reduced yields in the grain harvests and there were serious food shortages throughout England. The situation in Kent was made worse by continuing demand for grain from London, the capital being prepared to pay higher prices for foodstuffs than the local markets. Central government kept a close watch on the production and movement of grain throughout the county. A detailed document created by parish officials in 1596 for the Lord Lieutenant of Kent listed all farmers in Gillingham and Chatham. The record notes the size of the farming households, the amount of wheat, oats and barley they had sold, how much they had in store and what they intended to sow in the coming season. A second document records all the people in these two parishes who were said to be 'in want of corn'. The scale of the problem is evident: there were 511 people in Chatham and 466 in Gillingham identified as being in danger of going hungry that year.[14]

Wealthier individuals also felt the pinch as demands for taxation grew, food prices increased and rent payments fell. In the same year that labourer George Westill lost his rental income because of the plague, the Bishop of Rochester complained 'if there be no ease or abatement of our excessive payments, this extreme and terrible famine continuing … I must fain ere it be long to dissolve my house … send my servants a-begging, and my poor miserable neighbours a-starving'.[15]

Popular protest

Throughout early modern England, it was not unusual for those with a grievance to take to the streets. The Medway Towns were no exception to this. Popular protests relating to food supply and the payment of wages in Chatham Dockyard were evident in the early 1600s. In 1605 the movement of grain from farms to the riverside for export to Spain sparked a series of protests in the Medway area. On 20 February there were two separate incidents. Protesting crowds gathered in Gillingham and Chatham and the Gillingham mob became violent, attacking two men. A month later the ringleaders of each incident, all of them women, were brought before the Justices of the Peace at Rochester. They were charged with 'riotous assembly' and Agnes Bysley, Luce Woevenden and Ellen Markes from Gillingham stood accused of assault.[16]

Disputes about pay were a permanent feature of labour relations in the 17th-century English dockyard. Protests at Chatham Dockyard began in the 1620s and continued in various forms for the next two hundred years. The main problem was the delay suffered by workers in receiving their wages. The government was supposed to pay on a quarterly basis but in practice workers often had to wait years to be paid. To make matters worse, payment was not made in cash, but in the form of a ticket, which then had to be taken to the Navy Office in London and exchanged for cash. If workers needed cash they were either forced to sell their tickets at a loss to local creditors, or to supplement their income with some other form of employment.[17] In December 1626 shipwrights marched on the London offices of the Navy Board. They presented a petition which claimed that they had worked for a year:

> without a penny pay, neither having any allowance for meat or drink, by which many of them having pawned all they can, others turned out of doors for non-payment of rent, which with the cries of their wives and children for food and necessaries, doth heartily dishearten them.

The following year, workers who had not been paid for 18 months and whose boarding allowances had been stopped marched to London and laid siege to the Navy Board with 'neither clothes on their backs nor shoes'. Action brought little success. Although dockworkers were promised payment soon, by 1631 a total of £6,717 was still owed in arrears.[18]

The expanding townscape

The expansion of the workforce and of naval support services in Chatham Dockyard, combined with the installation of a resident Commissioner and other officials, created a demand for new residential building in Rochester and Chatham. The growing workforce which now began to settle locally could not be accommodated within existing housing stock. By 1600 the agricultural village of Chatham, which was clustered around the site of St Mary's church, began to expand southwards along the banks of a stream known as the Bourne or Brook. Smith's map of 1588 (Figure 25) shows that housing had also begun to stretch beyond Rochester's city walls to the east along the road towards Chatham.[19]

On the north side of the street leading away from the East Gate of the city of Rochester towards Chatham, a splendid Elizabethan town house was built in the 1580s for Sir Peter Buck following his appointment as Clerk of the Cheque in Chatham Dockyard. His Admiralty post gave him responsibility for the repair of ships and for building the storehouses required by the Navy at Chatham.

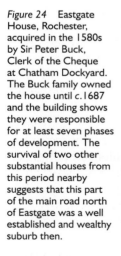

Figure 24 Eastgate House, Rochester, acquired in the 1580s by Sir Peter Buck, Clerk of the Cheque at Chatham Dockyard. The Buck family owned the house until *c*.1687 and the building shows they were responsible for at least seven phases of development. The survival of two other substantial houses from this period nearby suggests that this part of the main road north of Eastgate was a well established and wealthy suburb then.

Figure 25   Smith's map
of Rochester 1588: the
city is viewed from the
north. It also shows
Strood to the west, the
suburb beyond the city
walls at the Eastgate,
and St Mary's Church,
Chatham, to the east.

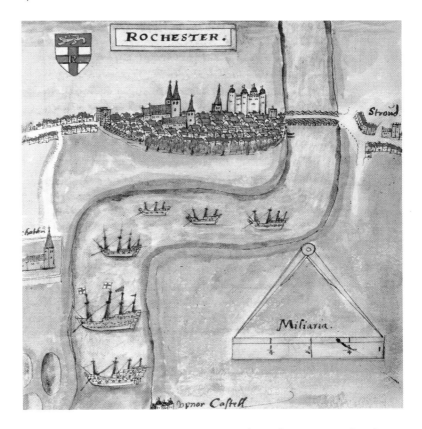

Figure 26   Detail of
a decorative ceiling in
Eastgate House, showing
the coat of arms of Sir
Peter Buck's second
wife, Mary Cresswell.
The ceiling is one of a
series with high-quality
plasterwork at the west
end of what was then a
very fashionable house.

The son of a wealthy Southampton merchant, he was not a local
man but became a respected member of local society. He was
elected mayor in 1593, served as an alderman throughout the rest of
his life and was also a warden of Rochester Bridge from 1602-24.[20]

Eastgate House was ideally situated for Buck's work, offering a
view of the ships on the Medway and easy access to the river by
boat across the adjacent marsh. Suitably impressive for a man of his
status, it was even thought good enough for royalty: in 1606 Buck
played host to the king of Denmark when he visited with James I to
inspect the navy. The house has two show fronts: one with jettied
storeys projecting over the high street and another – the main
entrance front with a magnificent display of fashionable polygonal
projections – set at right-angles to the street. Much of the original
interior has survived. In addition to extensive oak panelling and
two elaborately carved fireplaces, three rooms have intricately
decorated plaster ceilings which incorporate the coats of arms of
Sir Peter and his second wife.[21]

It was not only those with naval connections who established
a base for themselves in the city of Rochester at this time. Local
landowners found it useful to have a town house for business and

politics. William Paynter, Clerk of the Ordnance at the Tower of London, had bought the manors of Eastcourt, Twydall and Dane in Gillingham in the 1560s. The Paynter family maintained a country household at Twydall, and in 1617 William's grandson, also William, added to the family property with the purchase of 'a home or inn called the Kings Head with a tenement thereunto adjoining' in Rochester close to the market place. He then set about making improvements: 'The tenement was pulled down and new built and laid to the said inn anno 1617 when the great chamber was built.' At the same time he also leased two gardens and some waste land for a term of fifty years.[22]

LOCAL GOVERNMENT

The inhabitants of the Medway Towns were governed by several different bodies. Those who lived in Gillingham, Chatham and Strood remained under the authority of their respective parish councils and lords of the manor throughout the 17th century. In Rochester the parish authorities had a role to play but were overshadowed in civil matters by the city corporation. Both parish and corporation were rooted in the local community, but acted to administer national policies, such as the implementation of the Poor Laws, collecting taxes and maintaining roads. The presence of Chatham Dockyard imposed an additional authority in the Medway Towns in the form of the Navy Board. The board sat in London but was represented locally by the Commissioner, a post which became residential from 1630.[23]

The parish

Throughout England from the mid-16th century parish officials had an increasingly important role to play in the administration of local affairs. Elected by ratepayers, churchwardens reported on ecclesiastical matters and the overseers of the poor collected and administered the poor rate. They were also charged with preparing regular reports to central government on parish matters.

For example, in 1598 the overseers for Strood recorded a wealth of detail about the parish in response to a series of questions from the government. The document shows that the majority of the population were judged to be self-sufficient, with 97 rate-paying households and 30 households that neither paid rates nor took poor relief. A further 19 households were identified as being in the 'at risk' category, 'the poorer sort of people which are able to worke and doth neyther give nor take but if the husband should dye are liklie to be a parishe chardge'. The heads of households that did not pay rates were mostly unskilled labourers and sailors and the remainder were craftsmen such as carpenters, glaziers, tailors and glovers. Also listed are those who were currently 'relieved by the parish': three elderly widows and two lame men, a young orphaned brother and sister, and the unfortunate William Partington, aged 12, 'his toes rotted off'.[24]

Rochester Corporation

The most powerful authority in the Medway Towns at this time was the City of Rochester Corporation. In common with other towns with borough status, the freemen of Rochester sought to strengthen their position in the first half of the 17th century. This often resulted in a self-perpetuating and inward-looking corporation which restricted the number of new freemen. In 1625 the citizens of Rochester petitioned King Charles for confirmation and extension of their borough privileges. The new charter they were granted extended the boundaries of the city and changed the procedure for electing the mayor and aldermen.

The city limits were expanded to include part of Strood and those parts of the parish of St Margaret's that extended from the city walls along the main road to the boundary with the parish of Chatham, known today as St Margaret's Bank. This did not lead to a substantial influx of new freemen. Thomas Aukerson, a draper of St Margaret, and Robert Taylor, a turner from Chatham, were the first to take advantage of this new opportunity but between 1629 and 1662, of the 767 freemen's names entered in the city records, only 15 were listed as being from Chatham, 13 from St Margaret's and 18 from Strood. Between 1620 and 1659 on average only 14 new freemen were enrolled each year.[25]

The 1625 Charter also allowed changes in the election process for the mayor and aldermen. To calm the election process, which 'many times fall out to be tumultuous', entry to the ballot chamber was controlled and each freeman's vote was recorded. The number of mayoral candidates was reduced from all 12 aldermen to only two or three. Also, if a vacancy occurred among the aldermen in mid-term, a replacement was chosen by the remaining aldermen rather than by election. This made it easier for a family to retain office over several generations. For example, three generations of the Cobham family, owners of Temple Manor in Strood, served as mayor between 1599 and 1685 and Thomas Faunce senior was mayor in 1619 and his son Thomas in 1635.[26]

The physical presence of the city authorities was embodied in the Guildhall. The present building on the High Street, built in

1667, replaced an earlier building believed to have been further along the High Street on the site of the Corn Exchange. The importance of the mayor and corporation was also reinforced by civic ceremony, which became an increasingly important feature of town life throughout England in the late 16th and early 17th centuries. Rochester City accounts for 1591 record that £6 was paid to the 'goldsmith of Strowde' for '24 ounces of Sylver ... towards the mackinge of the great mace'. In the same decade the City minutes note that members of the corporation were asked to wear clothing appropriate to their status. That not all of them complied with this request is indicated by the repetition of this order in various guises throughout the 17th century. For example, in 1607 it was ordered 'that the said Mayor and his Bretheren upon everie Fryday beinge Lecture day shall decently come unto the Churche in theire gownes and ruffe bands and also upon everie Courte day'. In 1639 the spectacle of the mayor and aldermen parading the streets in their finery on feast days was reinforced by the decree that the civic regalia should be carried on these occasions. Those that mocked this public display of civic pride and authority were severely dealt with. In 1641 John Cobham, an alderman politically opposed to the mayor, was dismissed from the council when he sent William Streaton around 'all the taverns in Rochester in a Gowne with a white staffe in his hands in imitacion & derision of the said Maior'.[27]

The Navy Board

The Navy Board, established in 1546, was responsible for the administrative affairs of the naval service, including the building and repair of and supplies to naval ships throughout England. The Board sat in London but was represented in Chatham by a Commissioner and by the officers of the Royal Navy. The main concern of the Board was the maintenance of the fleet and the defence of the realm. Chatham Dockyard and its administration were set apart from the rest of the Medway Towns and the Admiralty gave naval officers exemption from holding local office. Nevertheless, navy men lived in the Medway Towns and some served as parish officers and others became honorary freemen of Rochester. The corporation also had an expectation that naval officers would adopt a responsible attitude in their dealings with the local community. In 1634 Philip Ward, mayor of Rochester, complained to the Navy Board that 'divers Navymen inhabit the city and misuse said liberty'. Exemption from public office was one thing but the corporation felt that these men had taken their freedom from responsibility a step too far: 'they misconstruing

think themselves free from contributing to any common charge in
that place where they live'.[28]

AGRICULTURE

Although much local employment was supported by the river,
with dockyard work, sailing and fishing providing employment
for many, most of the population was employed in agriculture for
at least part of the year. In 1596 there were 24 farming households
in Gillingham containing 253 people, and in Chatham there were
nine farming households with a total of 93 inhabitants. These large
households, with an average of nine to ten people in each, would
have contained the farmer, his family and servants and agricultural
labourers. There were also many smaller households of four to five
people, working a small plot of land and raising a few chickens and
sheep or pigs for their own use and combining this with fishing
or working in Chatham Dockyard. The practice of combining
occupations is evident from the property local people left in their
wills. For example, when John Punnett of Strood died in 1632
he left a fishing boat, 'a ketch called the Hanna', two small boats
with all the related nets and anchors, as well as several houses in
the village and surrounding area with barns, orchards, marsh and
arable land attached to them.[29]

Records kept by the Paynter family for Twydall Manor in
Gillingham give a clear picture of crops, land use and agricultural
practices in Gillingham in the late 16th and early 17th centuries.
A survey made of the manorial land in 1577 noted that the manor
house was surrounded by fruit trees: 'the great orcharde towarde
the north and the cherries garden towards the south' and 'One
great orchard sett with peare trees and aple trees and the northend
with cherrie trees'. A hop garden was added in 1631. Barley and
oats were staple grain crops and grass meadows produced hay as
winter feed for livestock. Wood was also a valuable commodity,
with woodland at Hempstead and elsewhere being coppiced and
used for fuel, charcoal and fencing.[30]

The use of marshland was an important aspect of agriculture in
Gillingham in the 17th century. Sea marsh was subject to tidal ebb
and flow but land was recovered by building tall thick banks from
mud, clay and river deposits, known locally as 'stuffe', around areas
of sea marsh. In time these areas, known as 'innings', drained and
pasture grew. The mud wall built around the innings was subject to
constant erosion and Paynter's records show the need for regular
repairs. Payments to 'scavelman' or ditch-digger Caswell in 1626
signal the building of a new inning called Lamb Hope. A year
later William Adcock was hired to repair the inning wall, making

it two yards deep and two feet high. When describing work on
the marshlands at Eastcourt, Paynter noted that he had agreed an
exchange of land with a neighbour, 'whereby I can be much better
supplied with stuff to mend my said inning wall on any occasion'.[31]

Between 1580 and 1640 the Medway Towns really began to feel
the effects of the establishment of Chatham Dockyard. Prompted
by the needs of national defence the communities began to change
and grow to accommodate the Navy, its personnel and ever-
increasing numbers of dockyard workers. The growth was patchy.
A flurry of activity in the dockyards in the 1580s was followed
by twenty years of stagnation in which Rochester, Chatham,
Gillingham and Strood all suffered from the disease and food
shortages of the 1590s. The threat of Dutch invasion reinvigorated
the dockyards in the 1620s and a new period of building and
growth began. Compared to what was to come in the next forty
years, which saw civil war, plague and a Dutch invasion, this
was a relatively calm and prosperous period in the history of the
Medway Towns.

Chapter 3

Destruction, disease and the Dutch invasion, 1640-80

Figure 27 The Royal Charles built by master shipwright Peter Pett for Cromwell and named Naseby for the Parliamentary victory at this battle. The ship was renamed the Royal Charles after the Restoration and was the Royal Navy's flagship. Captured by the Dutch on the raid on the Medway in 1667 she was sold for scrap six years later.

The mid-17th century was an unsettled period for England, and the Medway Towns did not escape their share of the conflict, disease and drama suffered by the nation. The Civil Wars of the 1640s and '50s brought disruption and, in some years, violence to government, church and the daily lives of the inhabitants. After the return of Charles II to the throne in 1661, the internal politics of the towns regained some stability, but then the Medway area was badly affected by the Great Plague of 1665-6. Close on the heels of this outbreak of disease came the daring and highly successful Dutch raid on the Royal Navy ships in the Medway in the summer of 1667. While causing little damage on land, there was panic among the local population. The Dutch navy destroyed several ships of the English naval fleet and finally captured and carried off the flagship the *Royal Charles* as a trophy of war.

THE CIVIL WARS IN THE MEDWAY TOWNS

The English civil wars of the mid-17th century brought political, social and religious upheaval to England on and off for nearly twenty years. Long-running disputes between Parliament and Charles I over taxation and the exercise of power came to a head in the summer of 1642 and split the nation into two factions, Parliamentarians and Royalists. Traditionally historians have interpreted the county of Kent as being staunchly Royalist but more recently it has been argued that in the 1640s the county was dominated by a radical Parliamentary minority. This ruling group was overthrown at the end of the decade when many disillusioned Parliamentarians joined forces with the Royalists. The Medway Towns shared in the violence and political turmoil that this drawn-out conflict brought to the county.[1]

As Civil War began, securing the county of Kent was a priority for Parliament. Occupying a strategic maritime position close to London and offering easy access to the continent, Kent was also a source of essential supplies of food and timber to the capital. Several days before Charles I raised the royal standard at Nottingham on 22 August 1642, declaring war on Parliament, Colonel Edwyn Sandys and his troops set out from London and made their presence felt in Kent, seizing arms from Royalist supporters and making arrests. On 20 August they entered Rochester and secured the bridge and castle. Within a couple of days Chatham Dockyard and 3,000 pieces of ordnance had been surrendered to Parliament by the resident Commissioner Phineas Pett. Upnor Castle and two warships on the river, *Sovereign* and *Prince Royal,* were also taken into parliamentary hands.[2]

The Parliamentary troops met with little opposition in the Medway Towns, although the welcome was perhaps greater in Chatham than Rochester. According to the Parliamentary news sheet *Perfect Diurnall,* 'such was the love of those who lived in Chatham, manifested to us' but 'We cannot say we found such love in Rochester'. Another contemporary account found no lack of warmth in Rochester's welcome for Sandys and his men, who were said to have been received by the mayor and citizens 'with the greatest love and alacrity there might be'.[3]

There may well have been mixed feelings towards Parliamentary troops in Rochester, given that Colonel Sandys and his men were also responsible for the damage done to Rochester Cathedral. In churches and cathedrals throughout England Parliamentary troops, led by those who were puritan in their religious beliefs, destroyed many of the symbols of worship that had survived the Reformation. Conflicting reports of these acts of iconoclasm in Rochester were written at the time. According to the rather matter-of-fact account in the *Perfect Diurnall*, the troops:

> went to the Cathedrall about 9 or 10 of the clock, in the midst of their superstitious worship… they … marched up to the place where the Altar stood … First they removed the Table to its place appointed, & then tooke the seate which it stood upon being made of deale board, having two or three steps to goe up to the Altar, & brake that all to pieces … This being done they pluckt down the rails, and lefte them for the poore to kindle their fires.[4]

By contrast, the Royalist newssheet *Mercurius Rusticus* ran the headline 'The Cathedrall Church of Rochester violated' and told the story in a far more sensational style.

> They brake down the raile about the Lord's Table, or Altar … most basely reviled a now Reverend Prelate … they seized upon the Velvet Covering of the Holy Table, and in contempt of those holy Mysteries which were Celebrated on the Table, removed the Table it selfe into a lower place of the Church … they strowed the Pavement with the torne mangled leaves of the booke of Common-Prayer.

John Lorkin, the dean, was shot at and almost 'murdered…at the very Altar'.[5]

No puritan ministry was set up to replace the disbanded cathedral chapter and the cathedral building was neglected until the Restoration in 1660. During the 1640s and '50s it was used by the community as a 'tippling house' and a carpenter's workshop. Local people also recycled materials from the building. Lead was stolen from the roof and a local shoemaker, John Wyld, was said to have removed and sold the iron work from the tombs. Although the fabric of the church was damaged, local people took action to preserve some of the cathedral's treasures. The ancient book *Textus Roffensis* (Figure 28) is thought to have been in the safekeeping of Sir Roger Twysden of Royden Hall, Peckham, throughout the civil wars. He returned it to the cathedral in 1663. The cathedral organ was also removed and stored in a tavern in Greenwich, to be safely returned after the Restoration.[6]

There were changes in church personnel at parish level as a result of the Civil War. John Man, vicar of Strood, was evidently a Royalist supporter and was removed from office in 1643 'for that he is a common drunkard and frequenter of Alehouses and Taverns, drawing others to the same excess with him, and is a common

Figure 28   The *Textus Roffensis*, or 'The Book of the Church of Rochester'. This 12th-century illustrated manuscript book contains a collection of Anglo-Saxon laws and the earliest surviving cathedral registers.

swearer by bloudy oaths, and used to curse, and is a common quarreller and fighter and said "that he scorned the Parliament and that the Parliament-men were not Gentlemen of quality, and hath expressed great malignity against the parliament". Man's successor, Daniel French, 'a very pious man' and a supporter of Parliament, was subsequently ousted from office after the Restoration because of his Nonconformity.[7]

In the years following 1642 leaders of the local communities in Chatham and Rochester actively supported Parliament. In both towns money was raised to improve defences against the threat of a Royalist attack. In Rochester Postmaster Philpott examined mail from abroad as it passed through the town and intercepted Royalist messages, and it was claimed that the mayor, Philip Ward, detained an envoy of the French ambassador on his way to the king.[8]

The dockyard workers also supported Parliament, following the lead of the Pett family, but it appears that they fared no better with regard to the payment of wages under Parliamentary rule than they had done in previous years. In 1644 it was reported that 'the ship-keepers are ready to mutiny'. The Earl of Warwick told the House of Lords, 'The mariners will be forced to seek maintenance elsewhere; and if for livelihood they should repair to the enemy, a greater advantage will thereby be given to man and set forth against the Parliament those ships that be already under their power'. The situation had not improved by December of the following year. A petition from the dockyard officers to Warwick said of the workers, 'their wants have grown to an extremity that they cannot any longer subsist'.[9]

The Medway Towns remained heavily defended against the threat of Royalist attack throughout the 1640s, which meant that the local population suffered the expense and inconvenience of having troops billeted in their homes. Despite this the towns remained loyal to Parliament until 1647, but by 1648 opinion began to change. Throughout the county, resentment of the Kent County Committee grew. The Committee, made up of men who supported Parliament, controlled the county and was charged with ensuring Parliamentary troops were fed and armed. The continuing demands made on the population of Kent to house and feed this army provoked a countywide atmosphere of rebellion. Signs began to emerge of a rift between the Kent County Committee and the people of Rochester as rumours went round that there were to be more troops billeted in the city, the fourth intake in a year. Moreover, the fear was that these men would be used to suppress a Royalist uprising. The mayor wrote to the Committee expressing both his concerns and those of 'the common people' about the dangers and costs they had borne, and sought mediation to relieve them of their burden.[10]

At the same time a petition was circulated in Kent in May which attacked the County Committee. Eleven of the Rochester councillors signed and on 22 May the Committee stated that the city had 'openly declared for the Kinge'. Before long Rochester and Chatham were in the hands of Royalist troops, along with Faversham, Sandwich and Sittingbourne. Peter Pett, who had taken over from his father Phineas as resident Commissioner, held Chatham Dockyard for Parliament although Royalist forces seized three ships, *Sovereign*, *Prince* and *Fellowship*.

Ten thousand Kentish Royalist supporters, led by the Earl of Norwich, marched to Blackheath, but the uprising was quashed by a Parliamentary army led by Thomas Fairfax. The Parliamentary troops headed back into Kent on 31 May to deal with the rebels. One regiment went to Rochester with orders to secure the bridge.[11]

An eyewitness account, written the day after the Parliamentarians began their attempt to regain Rochester, began by describing the measures taken by the Royalists to defend the city:

> At Rochester they bestirred themselves to the utmost, to make their Fortifications good; drawing up the bridge, and casting up workes where the need was, & planted 4 piece of Ordnance at the bridge foot: they also planted 40 of their greatest pieces upon the workes neer the River, and about the town for the defence of themselves against the army.

The Parliamentary troops were said to have 'fought gallantly' and 'the Kentishmen also stood it out stoutly … and many men were slain on both sides, it is said about 500 … likewise many are dangerously wounded, & it is feared much bloud will be spilt before the bridge can be taken'. The Royalist defence of the bridge was initially successful but when news arrived of the Parliamentary victory at Maidstone on 2 June, the rebels fled to Gravesend, where they crossed the Thames and escaped into Essex. As they withdrew from the city they destroyed the drawbridge at the centre of Rochester Bridge, to stop Fairfax's army from following them. According to a supporter of Parliament,; 'the Towne were very glad they were gone Major Brown Govourner of Upnor Castle as they were upon their going away overturned their carriages of their ordnance, and the women of the Town helpt to throw down the workes'.[12]

In the aftermath of the rebellion it became clear that perhaps support for Parliament was less secure in Rochester and Chatham than had previously been assumed. Dockyard workers had been active in the rebellion and Peter Pett reported that 300 to 400 recently discharged sailors at Chatham had joined the defence of

Figure 29 Peter Pett, master shipbuilder and resident Commissioner of the Royal Dockyards at Chatham from 1647 to 1668. He was disgraced for failing to save ships during the Dutch raid on the Medway in 1667.

Figure 30 Rochester Bridge in *c*.1790 showing the central drawbridge. A previous one was destroyed by retreating Royalists in 1648 to delay pursuit by Parliamentary troops.

Rochester against Parliamentary forces. Support for the Royalists was also evident amongst the local elite. Eleven of the 23 Rochester councillors took part in the 1648 rebellion and although the four men seen as having taken the most active role were purged from the city council by an order of central government in early 1649, the rest continued in post. In the 1650s, during the rule of the

Commonwealth and Protectorate, in Rochester, as elsewhere in the county, the mood continued to swing in favour of the monarchy.[13]

After the death of Oliver Cromwell in 1658, Royalists began to plot to restore Charles Stuart to the throne, bringing him back from exile on continental Europe. Rochester, en route from Dover to London, was an obvious stopping point for the royal entourage when Charles finally landed in England in May 1660, and when he entered the city the streets were lined with crowds throwing flowers and herbs to greet the monarch. The mood in the council chamber was not as sweet. Ninety men from Chatham and Rochester were expelled from the ranks of the freemen of the city to purge the ruling elite of those that had supported Parliament.

Restoration House

During an overnight stay in Rochester Charles and his brothers were entertained in an imposing town house located just outside the south-eastern corner of the city wall. As a result of that royal visit the building has since become known as Restoration House. It had been created *c.*1600 by combining and remodeling two medieval buildings. The impressive mansion was home to the Clerke family, several of whom served as MPs for Rochester. During the 1640s it had been commandeered and occupied by Colonel Gibbon, Cromwell's representative in the south east of England.

Recent work at Restoration House has revealed the extent of the redecoration that was done to receive the royal guests. Perhaps in recognition of Charles' extended stay in France, during which he would have gained a taste for continental interior design, the house was lightened and brightened. Decorative paint effects such

Figure 31 Restoration House, Rochester. The mansion house lay to the south-east, just outside the city walls, and gained its name from the visit of Charles II there on his return to England in 1660.

Figure 32 Details of some of the redecoration thought to have been done to prepare Restoration House for the visit of Charles II in 1660. Clockwise from right: double doors cut in the existing panelled wall and given a marbled paint finish, creating an entrance to a room in which to receive guests; the cornice of the room called the King's Bedroom japanned in gold and black; a chimneypiece painted onto the wall around a fireplace.

as marbling and japanning were used on the walls, fireplaces and wood paneling, and rooms were opened up by inserting French doors into partition walls.

The house gained further fame in the 19th century when it became known that Charles Dickens based his description of Miss Havisham's neglected home in *Great Expectations* on Restoration House.

DISEASE

Scarcely had the Medway Towns recovered from the upheavals of the Civil War than the population suffered another blow as a severe outbreak of bubonic plague took hold. The Great Plague, as this came to be known, spread throughout England during 1665-6. It was the last major visitation of this killer disease in England, although plague was endemic throughout the 16th and 17th centuries. In Kent serious outbreaks had occurred in 1603 and 1625 but in between these more virulent attacks the disease was present somewhere in the county in most years. For example in 1647 the discovery of plague in Rochester prompted the mayor to try to prevent its spread by requesting that the parliamentary army should billet its troops elsewhere.[14]

News of the latest outbreak reached Rochester in the summer of 1665. On 14 July three women, Elizabeth Brown for Strood and Margaret Walker and Joan Griffin for the City of Rochester, were sworn in as 'searchers of dead corpses'. The searchers had the unenviable task of examining the bodies of all those who died to look for 'any tumours or swellings or unusual spots or tokens which you shall or may suspect or believe to be the plague or pestilence … So help you God'. When found, such evidence was to be reported to the mayor. The first recorded plague burial of this outbreak in the Medway area was at Chatham on 20 August 1665. By the late summer, the disease had spread to Rochester as well and was increasing 'very much'. Both these communities and other ports on the Thames and the Kent coast were said to be 'miserably infected'. Within a few weeks the disease reached Gillingham and the first plague burial took place there on 20 October 1665.[15]

Chatham was particularly badly hit by the disease. Of a total population of around 3,000, nearly 900 died of plague in 1665-6, with the highest concentration of deaths in the late summer of 1666, when there were up to 50 plague burials a week. On 16 August 1666 Sir Jonathan Mennes wrote to the Navy commissioners in London asking that the cash to pay wages at Chatham Dockyard should be sent by water 'to avoid infected places'. The point of this precaution is not clear as he added, 'The plague increases at Chatham. 30 died last week and 100 houses are infected, no order is preserved but sick and well promiscuously visit each other.'[16]

Part of the problem for Chatham was that it had grown rapidly from a village to a densely populated town. With increasing pressure to house dockyard workers and officials close to their place of work, new plots of land were turned from agricultural to residential use and new, often sub-standard, housing was put up quickly. This was less of a problem for the dockyard officials, who lived in comfortable houses in Smithfield Bank to the south-east of St Mary's church and within easy walking distance of Chatham Dockyard. Less prestigious housing for dockyard workers grew up close by along the banks of a stream called the Bourne, forming a street which became known as the Brook.

The opportunities for money-making in an area so convenient for Chatham Dockyard had been spotted earlier in the century by dockyard officials and local landowners. Phineas Pett, master shipwright, recorded in his autobiography that in 1616 he bought two plots of land on the Brook. In 1621 Reginald Barker, the owner of the manor of Chatham, who then lived in Rochester, demolished the manor house and sold off the surrounding manorial land as small building plots. By the 1650s the dean and chapter of Rochester cathedral saw the potential for increased income and leased out 20 acres of their land known as the Brookfield, located between the stream and St Mary's church, also

Figure 33　A page from the parish register of St Mary's church in Chatham listing the plague deaths recorded from March 1666 to February 1667.

in small plots. The housing built on all this newly available land was designed for money-making rather than comfort and hygiene and the Brook soon became overcrowded and disease-ridden, a problem that would continue until the 20th century.[17]

The population of Gillingham was more widely dispersed and, after two initial deaths in October 1665, there were no further recorded plague fatalities until July of the following year when there was a rapid escalation of the number of burials from the disease. Seventeen victims died in July, eight in August, four in September, six in October, with the last two deaths, Ellen and Richard Roberts, on 7 and 15 November respectively. The Roberts were not the only family to lose more than one member. James and Robert Packenham both died in July, as did George Brown and his wife. Mary and Margaret Hunt died on consecutive days in August.[18]

Although the plague was a major killer, it was not the only disease to have an impact on the population of the Medway Towns during the period. The coastal marshes on the banks of the Medway were renowned for their unhealthy air. Edward Hasted, the Kentish historian, commented at the end of the 18th century that:

> on the north side of the great road, leading from London to Dover … there is a long space of country, lying near the banks of the Thames and the Medway … in which the air is gross, soggy, and much subject to intermittents, owing to the large tracts of low, swampy, marsh grounds, among which there are such quantities of stagnating waters, as render the country near them exceedingly unwholsome, especially in the autumnal quarter.[19]

This view echoed the comments of the author Daniel Defoe, who, on his travels around the county, described the area as 'marshy and unhealthy, by its situation among the waters', adding that this discouraged the settlement of 'families of note' in the area. The 'unwholesome' and 'unhealthy' nature of the area can be attributed to the mosquitoes that flourished in the damp and marshy conditions and spread a form of malaria known as the 'Kentish agues'. Rochester was described as a city which 'besides being subject to diseases in common with others, hath two diseases more epidemical, namely the scurvey for one but the Ague in special'. In 1669 an apothecary named Nicolas Sudell claimed to have found a cure for the latter disease. Sudell set up shop in Rochester and also took his cures to Maidstone market every week.[20]

The seafaring population played a significant role in spreading disease in the Medway Towns. The busy wharves of the port of Rochester and Chatham Dockyard had a constantly changing population which, on occasion, brought disease to the local community. In 1655 the Admiralty ordered the inhabitants of Chatham, Rochester and Strood to provide shelter and care for 'a great number of seamen from the Sound ... ill with spotted fever'. Payment was promised to those that nursed the sick, who were probably suffering from typhus. Unfortunately two years later no payments had been received and many local people had caught the 'spotted fever' and died. The inhabitants petitioned the Admiralty, complaining that 'We lost many friends and relations by the disease, which grew very violent through the multitude of diseased seamen forced upon us. There has been £415 due to us for two years past. We have not received a penny and most of us are very poor. We beg payment.' In 1955 several skeletons were found on a building site on Broom Hill in Strood. The curator of Rochester museum speculated that these may have been victims of this outbreak of spotted fever.[21]

THE DUTCH WARS

Despite the upheavals of the Civil War and frequent outbreaks of disease, Chatham Dockyard continued to grow in importance during the 17th century. This was largely due to the increased strategic significance of the Medway which resulted from the dispute between England and the Netherlands. The 'Dutch Wars', which began in 1652 and continued in fits and starts until 1674, were essentially about trade. The Dutch were a successful trading nation with an active merchant fleet. England, fearing competition for its own sea-borne trade, tried to restrict the activities of Dutch traders in English waters. The first Anglo-Dutch War broke out following the Navigation Act of 1651, which reserved the right to import goods to England for English ships and it restricted the shipping of exports to either English merchant ships or those of the nation that was to receive the goods. The Act hit the Dutch traders hard and the first clash of the wars took place in the Channel in 1652.

Preparations for War

The Medway Towns began to reap economic benefit from this war even before it started. In anticipation of naval conflict with the Dutch, the government had begun a new programme of shipbuilding in an attempt to bring a somewhat neglected English

Figure 34 The diarist Samuel Pepys, who was a frequent visitor to Chatham in the 1660s in his capacity as Clerk of the Acts and later as Secretary to the Navy Board.

navy up to fighting strength. This costly exercise absorbed nearly half of the Commonwealth government's revenues between 1649 and 1660 and Chatham received the lion's share of that money. Unfortunately this boom was short-lived. When Charles II took to the throne in 1660 the fleet had been restored but the government was deeply in debt. Shipyard workers throughout England had not been paid for months and threatened mutiny. Taking advantage of a lull in the fight with the Dutch, plans for further naval expansion were cancelled. Instead, cash and effort were channelled into maintaining the existing fleet.[22]

The proximity of Chatham Dockyard to the Channel and the North Sea made it an ideal place from which to launch attacks on the Dutch fleet and to repair ships damaged in the fighting on these seaways. Samuel Pepys, who was clerk to the Navy Board, made several official visits to the yards in the early 1660s. His diary entries suggest that the dockyards were not ready for conflict On 4 August 1662 Pepys and resident Commissioner Peter Pett inspected the yards. Setting out at 4 a.m. they first went out to the guard ships, which Pepys commented were 'badly manned'. The next ship, *Sovereign*, was found to be 'in good order and very clean' but once again 'few of the officers on board'. The *Royal Charles,* the pride of the fleet, was no better. Pepys declared himself 'troubled to see her kept so neglectedly'. Preparedness on dry land was little better. A muster of the 'ordinary', those men responsible for repair of the warships when laid up in dock, revealed that there was 'great disorder by multitude of servants and old decrepid men' and Pepys described the state of the storehouses as 'very bad'.

A year later Pepys found that security was still somewhat lacking. 'I spent the whole night in visiting all of the ships, in which I find, for the most part, ne'er an officer aboard nor any men so much as awake.' Pepys questioned Pett's ability to maintain discipline in the yard. He was 'much dissatisfied, and more than I thought I should have been with Commissioner Pett, being, by what I saw since I came hither, convinced that he is not able to exercise the command in the Yard over the officers that he ought to do.' A month later, Pepys was still concerned, noting that he was 'troubled to see how backward Commissioner Pett is to tell any faults of the officers'.[23]

With the outbreak of the second Dutch War in 1665, plans were made to create a new naval dockyard at Sheerness and to build a new fort there to improve the Medway's defences. In Chatham Dockyard the workers threatened mutiny as they had not been paid. In November Pepys was told that Commander Middleton had taken action to prevent trouble:

A meeting arising in the yard for want of money, [he] seized a good cudgel out of the hands of one of the men and took more pains on the use of it than many business for the last 12 months; clapped 3 men in the stocks for some hours and from thence to prison, where they continue ... Has not been troubled since.

With around £18,000 owing in back wages the Navy Board begged the king for money to pay the men and to buy more stores to put them to work. Only £6,000 was forthcoming.[24]

The long-term impact of non-payment of wages on the pockets of shipyard workers is seen in their probate inventories. These records of a person's possessions at death show that most dockyard workers, whether they were skilled shipwrights or labourers, were owed considerable sums of money in wages. Richard Vaughan, a miller of Gillingham, died in 1665, and his possessions are listed as being 'two very small beasts and one old blind horse' valued at £3 10s. and £14 5s. 5d. 'more due to him by waiges for service by him performed as a scavilman in his Majesty's dockyard at Chatham'. Three out of every four Gillingham men who worked in the yard died with more than half of their recorded wealth owed to them by the naval authorities. The government debt was often large: when William Laramer died in 1712 he was owed £71 10s. The inventories also indicate that dockyard workers like Richard Vaughan often supplemented their wages with other land-based work.[25]

The Dutch raid

It was in this atmosphere of lax security and low morale that the attack on the Medway by the Dutch Navy took place in the summer of 1667. Following the defeat of the Dutch at the Battle of North Foreland in 1666, the two nations had entered into protracted peace negotiations. Preoccupied with the problems of the plague, the Great Fire of London and necessary economies, Charles II ordered the English fleet to be moored and their crews dismissed. The government assumed that the peace negotiations would be successful. Despite the warning of the danger of attack from the North Sea, uttered a half-century earlier by Admiral Monson, little attention was paid to the security of the fleet in the Medway.

Meanwhile, the Dutch planned their raid on the foremost English naval base. A direct attack on the English coast had been considered for some time but in the summer of 1666 English action on the Dutch coast strengthened their resolve. After a battle in the North Sea, Sir Robert Holmes carried out a raid on the Dutch coast in which 170 Dutch ships were destroyed by fire and the small and

undefended town of Westerschelling was plundered and burnt
to the ground, an attack which came to be known as 'Holmes'
bonfire'. Preparations for the attack on the Medway were thorough
and many English sailors with a good working knowledge of the
Medway were recruited from Dutch prisons to man the Dutch fleet
of over 80 vessels.

The Dutch raid on the Medway in June 1667 was swift and
effective. The weekend before the attack a Dutch squadron sailed
up the Thames as far as Canvey Island and set fire to buildings.
The same squadron, led by Vice Admiral Willem van Ghent,
then set off for Sheerness. On Monday 10 June the new fort at
Sheerness came under attack and by the end of the day, despite
the arrival of reinforcements, the English had abandoned the
fort to Dutch troops. On Wednesday 12 June Dutch ships sailed
up to Gillingham and attacked the English ships guarding the
defensive chain across the river from Gillingham to Hoo Ness. The
chain failed to hold back the invaders but, as the tide turned, they
anchored for the night.

On that day some of the sailors from the Dutch ships landed
at Gillingham. According to Pepys they behaved well. Given the
English actions in Westerschelling the previous year, he found it
'remarkable' that the Dutch troops 'killed none of our people nor
plundered our houses: but did take some things of easy carriage
and left the rest and not a house burned'. One recorded casualty of
this day was the bedding and linen of Henry Frewin. According to
the local men who listed his belongings after his death in January
1668, these household items were 'plundered by the duich att
the fight'.[26]

Meanwhile in Chatham there was panic and many of the
inhabitants fled. Peter Pett and other dockyard officials began to

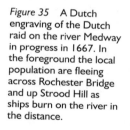

Figure 35   A Dutch
engraving of the Dutch
raid on the river Medway
in progress in 1667. In
the foreground the local
population are fleeing
across Rochester Bridge
and up Strood Hill as
ships burn on the river in
the distance.

Figure 36 The Dutch raid on the Medway, 1667. View looking south-west from Sheerness down the winding Medway towards Chatham and Rochester. In the distance are Rochester castle and cathedral, closer to the middle distance are the ships which were sunk to obstruct the Dutch. Just beyond them on the right is the captured *Royal Charles*. Further away on the right is Upnor Castle.

remove their personal possessions from the town at the first sign of trouble and much of what remained in Gillingham was plundered by Scottish troops brought in to help with the defence of the yard. Many of the dockyard workers also fled. Pett later said that 'of 800 men on pay in Chatham only about ten persons could be found at the crisis'. Pett failed to carry out an order to move ships upriver but the Duke of Albemarle, sent to organise the defence of the yards, set up a gun battery on the bank at Chatham and also sank three ships to form a defensive barrier.[27]

Despite Albemarle's actions, on 13 June the Dutch were able to sail upriver, burn three English ships and carry off the prestigious *Royal Charles* as a trophy. Rather than press their cause further and attempt to destroy Chatham Dockyard, the Dutch acknowledged their vulnerability and withdrew. Under constant attack from the battery at Upnor castle and having used up all their fire ships, they retreated victorious. As Pepys later reflected, their capture of the *Royal Charles* was a feat of daring done 'at a time, both for tide and wind when the best pilot in Chatham would not have undertaken it'.[28]

After the raid

This was a shameful defeat for the English and the search for a scapegoat began immediately. Three days after the departure of the Dutch, Peter Pett was arrested and sent to the Tower of London where he was held until December. Although he was blamed for the English defeat he escaped conviction. His punishment was to be dismissed from his post as Commissioner of Chatham Dockyard in February 1668.

Figure 37 The fort at Gillingham, built to improve defences after the Dutch raid.

As Pett was arrested some of those wounded in the defence of Chatham Dockyard died. The parish register for Gillingham recorded the burial of 'Fox a soldier' on 17 June and of Jeremiah Howard 'a soldier' five days later. Other wounded men lingered for some weeks, with five more military burials recorded in late August and early September.[29]

In the aftermath of defeat the authorities recognised the need to improve the Medway's defences. Forts were built at Sheerness, Gillingham and Cockham Wood, the chain across the river at Gillingham was replaced and new gun emplacements were installed on the riverbanks. Fortunately this line of defence was not tested again. The events on the Medway in the summer of 1667 were the last major hostilities of the second Dutch War, which ended on 31 July with the Treaty of Breda. Although conflict began again between the English and the Dutch in the third Dutch War of 1672-4, the Medway Towns suffered no further indignities as Chatham Dockyard continued to build and repair ships for the navy.

The disruption of 20 years of political upheaval followed by the disgrace of the Dutch attack has left few traces on the landscape of the Medway Towns today. Carpenters and tipplers were ejected from the cathedral, the altar rails were replaced and it once again became a place of worship. On Rochester Bridge the drawbridge was rapidly repaired after the retreat of the Royalists in the 1648 rebellion. The new fort built at Gillingham to improve the dockyard defences has not survived and there is now no chain across the Medway to prevent incoming ships. Upnor Castle, built as a gun fort by Queen Elizabeth, was downgraded in 1668 to a magazine, supplying powder and shot to warships in the river. It now provides 21st-century tourists with a reminder of the ignominious defeat of the English Navy by the Dutch in 1667.

Figure 38 Upnor Castle, a rare example of an Elizabethan artillery fort, was built in 1559 and enlarged later to protect the warships in the nearby dockyards. It failed to do that when the fleet at anchor was burned by the Dutch in 1667 and so, from 1668, it was no longer maintained for defensive purposes. Instead it was used to store supplies of powder and shot for warships.

Chapter 4

Commercial battles and fine buildings, 1680-1720

In the late 17th century there was no doubt in the minds of visitors that the Medway area was defined by the river and by the intense activity in Chatham Dockyard. When Celia Fiennes visited in the 1690s the land-based wonders of the city of Rochester merited little more than a passing reference. The cathedral was dismissed as 'a good building but nothing Curious' and the castle passed over as 'a pretty Little thing'. The river and Chatham Dockyard received far more attention. She declared the river Medway to be 'the finest River I ever saw'. Rochester Bridge was enthusiastically described as 'the finest in England – nay its said to Equal any in the world … its very long and fine'. She went on to describe the 'two large yards for building shipps', including the mast pond. Gillingham, lying some distance from the main road, does not feature in her account and to her eyes Chatham and Strood, the ships and Chatham Dockyard were all part of Rochester. Her description suggests the emergence of an urban conurbation: 'The town is large includeing the suburbs and all, for there is a large place before you pass the river which washes quite round that side of the town to the Dockyards, that's a mile from it.'[1]

Figure 39   The Medway in 1690, looking south towards Rochester and Chatham and showing how the two communities had been almost joined together by building. The extent of Chatham Dockyard can be seen on the riverbank to the left of the picture.

When Daniel Defoe arrived in the Medway Towns some thirty years later, he was more aware of the separate communities of Chatham, Rochester and Strood. He emphasised that they were 'three distinct places, but contiguous, except the interval of the river between the two first, and a very small marsh or vacancy between Rochester and Chatham'. He shared Fiennes' views on the contrast between the old city of Rochester and the exciting bustle of shipbuilding and naval stores.

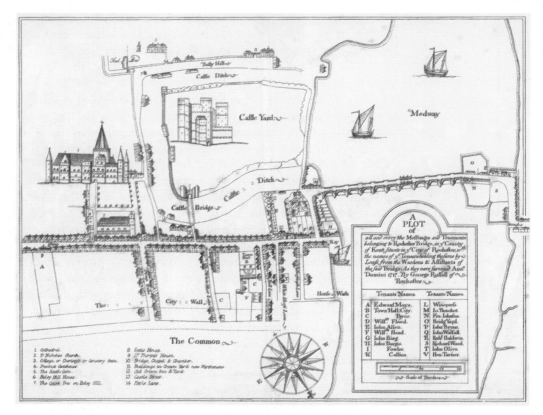

Figure 40 George
Russell's map of
Rochester, 1717, made
to record the land
and buildings owned
by Rochester Bridge
Trust and the names
of the tenants of these
properties. It shows
how most of the built-up
area was north of the
main road. It also shows
Rochester's quay, 'Kay'
on the riverbank to the
north of the bridge.

There's little remarkable in Rochester, except the ruins of a
very old castle, and an ancient but not extraordinary cathedral;
but the river, and its appendices are the most considerable of
the kind in the world. This being the chief arsenal of the royal
navy of Great-Britain. The buildings here are indeed like the
ships themselves, surprisingly large, and in their several kinds
beautiful: The ware-houses, or rather streets of ware-houses,
and store-houses for laying up the naval treasure are the largest
in dimension, and the most in number, that are any where to
be seen in the world: The rope-walk for making cables, and the
forges for anchors and other iron-work, bear a proportion to
the rest; as also the wet-dock for keeping masts, and yards of the
greatest size, where they lye sunk in the water to preserve them,
the boat-yard, the anchor yard; all like the whole, monstrously
great and extensive, and are not easily describ'd.[2]

The physical growth of both Rochester and Chatham was
shaped and, to a certain extent, constrained by the topography.
The 1717 map of Rochester shows an unbroken line of buildings
from the river to the city gates along the main London to Dover

road. Most of the building off the main thoroughfare was on the flat land to the north of the road, stretching down to the marshland beside the river. The land to the south, behind the cathedral and castle, was steep and wooded and less easy to build on. The Hearth Tax assessments of the 1660s and '70s suggest that the wealthiest members of the population of Rochester lived to the south of the main road in the area around the cathedral. The central main road was also the commercial centre of Rochester and in the late 17th and early 18th centuries the new civic building, the Guildhall, was constructed on the north side of the road.[3]

During this period there was also substantial expansion and rebuilding in Chatham Dockyard and in the village of Chatham as it grew to accommodate the resident workforce. With the dockyard occupying the prime building land to the north of the old village centre, the steep wooded hills that overlooked this area, although not ideal for building, were used to accommodate the workers. Celia Fiennes mentioned that in the area around Chatham Dockyard, 'here are severall streetes of houses on this hill which is pretty high', and commented that 'on the hill you have the best prospect of the town'.[4]

Although contemporaries sometimes failed to notice the physical divisions between the Medway Towns, records from the end of the 17th century show that Rochester, Chatham, Gillingham and Strood were four very different places. It was also during this period that rivalry between Rochester and Chatham gathered pace. The competition for economic and political supremacy between the ancient cathedral city and the new industrial town, which began in the 1680s with a dispute over market rights, continued throughout the 18th and 19th centuries. As the Royal Naval Dockyards continued to grow and Chatham's population increased dramatically, Rochester's pre-eminence at the mouth of the Medway was severely tested.

The dispute over Chatham market

Since the incorporation of Rochester in 1464, the city had the right to hold fairs and markets within the city walls and to collect tolls and dues on the goods sold. Towards the end of the 17th century this economic advantage was challenged. There were two sources of concern. The first, beyond Rochester's control, was the growth of Maidstone as a market town, offering an alternative outlet for the sale of goods from north-west Kent. The second, closer to home, was the establishment of a market in Chatham. The population of the dockyard town was expanding rapidly. Between 1680 and 1720 the number of dockyard workers grew and the population more than doubled, rising from around 2,100 to c.5,000, making it similar in size to Rochester. Chatham had no ancient right to hold a market but in the 1660s a market sprang up within the dockyard, saving the workers and their families the trouble of walking to Rochester to buy food. This initiative was a source of considerable irritation both to the Rochester corporation and to traders in the city. The market dispute dragged on for the next forty years and foreshadowed the struggle for political and economic dominance that would colour relationships between Rochester and Chatham for the next two centuries.[5]

At first sight, it appears Chatham was at a considerable political disadvantage in the struggle over the market. Rochester held a charter which gave them the right to hold a market and a corporation to protect these rights. Chatham, despite its population growth, continued to be administered by the parish vestry of St Mary's church. This group of local men, presided over by the churchwardens, met irregularly and had no authority over the development of the town. However, the vestry had two allies in this dispute. Both Sir Oliver Boteler, the lord of the manor of Chatham, and the Admiralty had an interest in exerting their influence on behalf of the dockyard town.[6]

The first move made by the freemen of Rochester, most of whom were shopkeepers and traders who feared the loss of revenue that the Chatham market threatened, was to attempt to gain political control over the dockyard town. In 1674 they began legal proceedings in Parliament, arguing that Chatham market contravened Rochester's charter and seeking to remedy this by bringing Chatham under their jurisdiction. This manoeuvre was blocked by the Admiralty's opposition to an extension of Rochester's powers over the dockyard town.[7]

Sir Oliver Boteler then stepped in. He went directly to Charles II and was granted the right to hold a Saturday market and an annual fair on his manorial land in the centre of Chatham. There was no consultation with the city of Rochester and they retaliated by taking action against Boteler, claiming that he had misled the Crown. The legal wrangling continued for several years. In 1686 an inquiry heard the evidence of 40 witnesses and concluded that the grant should be revoked, as Chatham fair and market were not in the interests of the city of Rochester. When Boteler's appeal against this decision failed, he organised a petition from the people of Chatham. Once again the Navy Board was consulted. They were of the opinion that the granting of a fair and market in Chatham 'would be a great convenience and relief to the inhabitants of Chatham who are now becoming very numerous but likewise great advantage to H M Service'. James II approved the grant of the market and, despite Rochester corporation continuing to appeal, the grant was confirmed by William III in 1689. This dispute cost the city of Rochester over £1,000 in legal fees and had brought them no gain. The people of Chatham enjoyed the advantage of their own market for the next 20 years.[8]

This was not the end of the matter for the freemen of Rochester. In 1710 they seized an opportunity offered by their newly elected MP, Admiral Sir John Leake, who was also the chairman of the Navy Board, to revisit the dispute. Leake was asked, with 'almost near unanimity', that he should 'use his endeavours to put down Chatham market'. While the city lawyers prepared the evidence for legal proceedings, a committee was set up to consider other possibilities. They decided to revive the idea of incorporating Chatham into the jurisdiction of the city of Rochester. Mayor John Unite, claiming that the initiative had come from some residents of Chatham, suggested that the boundaries of the city of Rochester should be extended to include all the charity lands that the corporation owned in Chatham and that a new market should be sited on this land. This would ensure the city received the dues on goods sold and have the additional bonus of requiring all traders, formerly of Chatham but now resident in Rochester, to purchase the freedom of the city to sell their wares within its newly extended boundaries.[9]

The plan was discussed with six leading citizens of Chatham and Strood at the *Bull Inn* on 2 March 1711 and a cautiously favourable response was brought to Rochester council the following day. The Rochester aldermen were strongly opposed to the plan. They feared that their own trade would suffer and the meeting ended in uproar with no agreement reached. The legal route to suppress the market was also abandoned when Leake's legal counsel advised the city that a market of twenty years' standing would be difficult to suppress. Rochester had lost the battle with its neighbour for control of trading in the Medway Towns.[10]

Building in Chatham Dockyard

The main reason for the dramatic increase in Chatham's population was the continuing expansion of Chatham Dockyard, which by the early 1700s employed over a thousand men. The increase in the size of the workforce was prompted by warfare at sea. The Anglo-Dutch wars had ended in 1674, but were soon followed by war with France in 1689-97, with Spain from 1702-13 and the Jacobite rebellions of 1715-19. Conflict meant that the demand for warships was high and national expenditure on the dockyards averaged more that £1 million per year between 1688 and 1711. To help meet the demand, Chatham Dockyard was expanded and there was much new building on the site.

Figure 41 The
Commissioner's House,
Chatham Dockyard,
built 1703, the oldest
intact naval dockyard
building in England, sited
in the centre of the early
18th-century Dockyard
on the site of the home of
earlier commissioners.

Figure 42 The main
gate in the protective
wall round the dockyard.
Wall and gate were built
in 1716-20 in the style
used by the Board of
Ordnance at Woolwich
Arsenal on the Thames.
The gate towers provided
accommodation for the
Yard porter and the
boatswain. George III's
coat of arms was put
there in 1812 when the
original arms were moved
to the north side.

In 1685 new land was bought for the yard which increased the
dockyard's river frontage to over 1,000 yards. Two new dry docks
were commissioned to meet the requirement for larger warships.
One was to be built by dockyard workers and the other was
put out to a private contractor. Samuel Pepys wrote to the Navy
Commissioners in 1685 recommending that John Rogers, house
carpenter, be paid £5,310 in instalments for the building of one of
the dry docks. Rogers evidently did a satisfactory job as a couple
of years later he was also paid to build a storehouse.[11]

The 1680s also saw the building of a large brick storehouse at a
cost of over £5,000, 10 mast houses and, on reclaimed marshland,
a new mast pond and mast house. The mast pond was described
by Celia Fiennes on her visit to Chatham, who observed that
'there was in one place a sort of arches like a bridge of brick-work,
they told me the use of it was to let in the water there and so they
put their masts into season'. The work of improvement continued
in the 1690s with new workshops for painters, smiths and oar-
makers, a new forge and new cranes on the waterfront. By the end
of the 17th century, Chatham was better equipped for the building
of warships than any other English dockyard.[12]

Facilities within Chatham Dockyard were also improved
during the first twenty years of the 18th century and much of the
building from this period still stands. The Commissioner's House
was built in 1703 to meet the demands of Captain George St Lo
when he took up post as resident Commissioner. St Lo was used
to a grander living accommodation in Plymouth and declared the
existing residence, built in the 1640s for Phineas Pett, below the
standard he required.

Between 1716 and 1720 a wall was built around Chatham Dockyard. The finishing touch to this new security measure was the imposing main gate with its towers and grand archway. Within the yards a new ropery was built in 1719 and a multi-purpose building was constructed in the 1720s. The latter (called the Clocktower building) had on the ground floor six bays which were left open and used as saw pits, a top floor or mould loft, used for laying out the plans of ships, and in the rest of the building was a 'present use store', for materials for ships being built or repaired.

The range and complexity of the dockyard enterprise is evident from Defoe's description.

> We come next to the stores themselves … The sails, the rigging, the ammunition, guns, great and small-shot, small-arms, swords, cutlasses, half pikes, with all the other furniture belonging to the ships that ride at their moorings in the river Medway: These take up one part of the place, having separate buildings, and store-houses appropriated to them, where the furniture of every ship lies in particular ware-houses by themselves, and may be taken out on the most hasty occasion without confusion, fire excepted.
>
> Besides these, there are store-houses for laying up the furniture, and stores for ships … For this purpose there are separate and respective magazines of pitch, tarr, hemp, flax, tow, rosin, oyl, tallow; also of sail cloth, canvas, anchors, cables, standing and running rigging, ready fitted, and cordage not fitted; with all kinds of ship-chandlery necessaries, such as blocks, tackles, runners, &. with the cooks, boatswains, and gunners stores, and also anchors of all sizes, grapnells, chains, bolts, and spikes, wrought and unwrought iron, cast-iron work, such as potts, caldrons, furnaces, &. also boats, spare-masts and yards; with a great quantity of lead and nails, and other necessaries, (too many to be enumerated) whose store looks as if it were inexhaustible.[13]

Figure 43 The Clocktower Building, the oldest surviving store in any English royal dockyard, was built in 1723 of timber above a brick ground floor, partly open to the saw pit. It was rebuilt and the upper storeys encased in brick in 1802.

Figure 44 Rochester's former Guildhall and Court as built in 1687 (left), was a free-standing building with a court chamber above an open ground floor and a council chamber over the rear staircase. After 1830 it was gradually enlarged and embellished to house municipal offices and is now home to the Guildhall Museum.

There was also an expansion of the facilities for preparing and storing the food for the warships' crews. The victualling yard was on the riverbank to the west of Chatham Dockyard, on the border between Rochester and Chatham. New land was leased from St Bartholomew's hospital in 1695 to establish a new office, and new stores were established in the early 1700s.[14]

Civic building in Rochester

Rochester experienced little growth in this period but there was some prestigious new civic building in the city. In 1687 the Guildhall was erected, on what is now Rochester High Street, to replace an earlier building sited further to the east. The initiative to build the hall began in March 1686 when the mayor, John Bryan, bought the leasehold of the land and the houses on it from Sir Richard Head on behalf of the corporation. The land itself belonged to the Rochester Bridgewardens. Unfortunately the corporation did not have enough money to pay for the lease, the demolition of the existing houses and the building of the Guildhall, probably as a result of the legal expenses it incurred trying to prevent the market in Chatham. Mayor Bryan and the other aldermen agreed 'to use their utmost endeavours to gather all such money as any person shall think fit to give and contribute' towards the proposed building, with any shortfall in funds from donations to be met by the corporation. By February of the following year the work was complete. The corporation minutes noted that the unfortunate Mayor Bryan 'hath expended a considerable sum of money more than he hath received'. £200 of his own money was never repaid.[15]

The Guildhall provided a meeting place for the city council, and was also used as a courthouse for the assizes. The forecourt of the building offered a public space; when William Hogarth and his friends visited the Medway Towns in 1732 they 'played at hop scotch in the colonnade under the town hall'. Inside, the highly decorated plaster ceilings over the main staircase and council chamber were paid for by the local MP Admiral Sir Cloudesley Shovell. Shovell served as MP for Rochester from 1698 to 1701 and from 1705 until his death in 1707.[16]

Like most MPs of the day he spent very little time in his constituency, but he did spend money in the city to ensure

Figure 45   The ceiling of the former court chamber in the Guildhall, with decorative plasterwork paid for by Sir Cloudesley Shovell. The room has fine contemporary fittings.

Figure 46   The elaborate façade of the Corn Exchange on Rochester High Street, built in 1706. Behind it there are only fragments of the original building, which was replaced in 1870 with a new exchange facing Northgate.

Figure 47 Admiral Sir Cloudesley Shovell was MP for Rochester 1698-1701 and 1705-7. While in office, he paid for decorative features in the newly built Guildhall and for the building of the Corn Exchange.

that he remained in favour with the voters. In 1706 he paid for the building now known as the Corn Exchange on the High Street to the east of the Guildhall and for the subsequent addition of a town clock. On one of the rare occasions that Sir Cloudesley Shovell did visit Rochester, he was treated to a lavish meal by the mayor. The City records for September 1701 include a bill for £15 2s. which paid for bread and beer, beef, fowl, geese, two pigs, a leg and shoulder of mutton, pigeon pie, apple pies and mince pies, washed down with over £9 worth of wine and accompanied by a good fire and plenty of tobacco.[17]

LIFE IN THE LOCAL COMMUNITY

Commenting on the whole north Kent coast, Daniel Defoe was in little doubt as to the inferiority of society to be found on the waterside at the turn of the 18th century. Compared with Maidstone, where it was possible to 'converse with gentlemen, and persons of rank of both sexes, and some of quality', or the Medway valley 'spangl'd with populous villages, and delicious seats of the nobility and gentry', the towns bordering the Thames and Medway estuaries were described as a social wasteland in an area that was 'marshy, and unhealthy, by its situation among the waters'. In Defoe's view, these riverside communities were 'embarass'd with business, and inhabited chiefly by men of business, such as ship-builders, fisher-men, seafaring-men, and husband-men, or such as depend upon them, and very few families of note are found among them'.[18]

The social and economic dominance of trades and crafts in the Medway Towns at this time is evident from the occupations of the mayors of Rochester. Between 1701 and 1760, 34 men held this office and only three were listed as gentlemen and one as esquire. The rest were drawn from the craftsmen and tradesmen of the city: carpenters, grocers, bakers, tailors and surgeons led the corporation.[19]

Typical of the 'middling sort' of residents to be found in Chatham were the grandparents of the Kent county historian Edward Hasted. Joseph Hasted was a painter in Chatham Dockyard, one of the more prestigious trades, and made enough money to buy a townhouse in Chatham 'at the corner of King Street on Smithfield Bank over the Brook there', an area that housed many dockyard officials and more prosperous skilled workers. As a freeholder in the town from 1707, he served on the quarter sessions jury and was high constable from 1710-11. Hasted's account of their life suggests that it was comfortable, convivial and relatively privileged for the growing community of Chatham:

> Being looked on at Chatham as very rich, they were looked on accordingly with much respect. Their housekeeping was exceedingly plentiful, but their visitors who partook of it were in general their relations, according to the fashion of the time; their hours were early, they rose in the morn at 5 o'clock and played together at backgammon till breakfast at 8 o'clock. They had at morn some thick cake and mead, they dined at 12, drank tea at 4, and supped at 8. He brewed his own beer, which he prided himself much in, especially his strong beer, which he kept to the age of several years. Their beverage after dinner was elder wine, which, as well as several other sorts, she made herself being an excellent housewife.[20]

Evidence from probate inventories

Further details of the prosperity, possessions and living conditions of this 'middling sort' of people emerge from probate inventories. These documents record the name and often the occupation of the deceased followed by a detailed list of the goods they owned and debts outstanding to them at the time of their death. The record was made by appraisers who noted not only what possessions they found in the home of the deceased but also which room they found them in, providing clues about accommodation and the layout of homes. These snapshots of the material circumstances of individuals exclude the poorest and the wealthiest and focus on those whose probate inventory was registered in the local church courts, the skilled artisans, tradesmen, shopkeepers and those with modest agricultural holdings.[21]

Wealth

There is a marked contrast in the levels of prosperity to be found in the urbanised communities of Chatham, Rochester and Strood compared with the rural village of Gillingham (Figure 48). In the three towns 16 per cent of inventories showed assets worth over £300 but in Gillingham only seven per cent enjoyed this level of wealth.

Figure 48 Table showing the value of goods and effects listed in probate inventories in the Medway Towns (1667-1783).

Location	Value of goods and effects			
	£1-300	£300-1,000	£1,000+	Total
Chatham, Rochester and Strood	432 (84%)	75 (15%)	6 (1%)	513 (100%)
Gillingham	108 (93%)	4 (7%)	0 (0%)	112 (100%)

The communities also differed in the occupational groups who enjoyed a higher level of wealth. In Gillingham, the four men whose goods were worth over £300 were all working in the agricultural sector: a miller, two yeomen and a farmer. In Chatham, Rochester and Strood, only about a quarter of this wealthiest group gained their wealth from agriculture and all the other major occupational groups were represented: dockyard workers, seamen, tradesmen, craftsmen and professionals could all make an excellent living in and around the early 18th-century town.

Occupations

Nearly a third of all those whose goods were assessed relied directly on the river Medway for their livelihood but the balance of occupation was different in each of the four communities. In Chatham around one in three worked in the dockyard. Those from further afield were less likely to be dockworkers, only one in six in Gillingham, one in 11 in Rochester and there is no evidence of men travelling the two miles to the yards from Strood. Those that did work in Chatham Dockyard were not always exclusively employed there, probably a reflection of the government's habit of keeping their employees in arrears with wages. For example, William Mitchell, a shipwright of Gillingham, died in possession of a barn full of barley, peas and hay, eight acres of wheat ready for ploughing in the fields, eight cows and four pigs. Although the barley was his most valuable asset worth £47, the 'wages due and oweing ... for his service performed in her majesties Dock Yard in Chatham' came a close second, totalling £45 2s.[22]

While most dockyard workers were based in Chatham or Gillingham, Strood is where the greatest concentration of fishermen was found. The majority were of moderate means, owning a single fishing boat and perhaps a smaller cock boat, a kind of dinghy, and a few household items. The three fishermen from Gillingham were of similarly modest means. John Snoborne combined fishing with ropemaking, leaving '2 smacks & an open cock & a skille with all dredges and anchors and furniture thereunto belonging', valued at £35.[23]

Rochester was the customs port for the Medway estuary, and many of the traders who imported and exported goods were based in the city. Coal and salt were brought in from the north east of England, and cargoes of dairy produce, wine, tobacco and manufactured goods were imported from London to supply the local markets. Outgoing shipments of oats and barley were taken to London and there was some export of oysters overseas. Ships were

Figure 49　A hoy, a small single-masted cargo or passenger boat.

registered in Rochester, Chatham and Strood. Various small vessels such as lighters, hoys and barges were owned by those engaged in trade in and out of the Medway, transporting coal, ballast, chalk, lime and foodstuffs.[24]

As with any sizeable urban community at this time, the conurbation of Strood, Rochester and Chatham was home to a wide range of traders and craftsmen making personal items. Innkeepers, vintners, victuallers and other suppliers of foodstuffs were among the wealthiest townsmen, supplying the navy and the dockyard workers as well as the local community. The clothing needs of the population were met by haberdashers, tailors, cordwainers and a glover. Rochester was home also to a range of specialist retailers such as apothecaries, barbers, booksellers and tobacconists.

Retail trade in Gillingham was less diverse and the traders were less wealthy. The village boasted a butcher and a shopkeeper. Details in the inventory of widow Anne Foote suggest that her store aimed to cater for most of the daily needs of the villagers. She stocked a wide range of goods: foodstuffs, kitchen and household items, clothes, shoes, household linen and haberdashery and a few primers and books. Despite this impressive offering, trading had not made her particularly rich. The total value of all her possessions including the shop stock came to little more than £50. There was also evidence of some small-scale brewing in Anne's washhouse. Many householders had a brew-house attached to their home, with the equipment for producing beer on a small scale for domestic consumption.

There is a similar contrast between the three towns and Gillingham in respect of the artisans and craftsmen operating in each. The towns provided occupation for those working in the building trades, such as carpenters, brick makers and layers, joiners and glaziers. The brewing trade needed coopers to make barrels and there was plenty of work for craftsmen who supported transport, such as wheelwrights, blacksmiths and saddlers. Tanners and curriers provided the leather for saddles and shoes. Some of these craftsmen became very wealthy and influential. For example, one currier died with property worth over £700 and, as we have seen, many artisans and traders rose to hold political office.[25]

In Gillingham there were fewer craftsmen offering a narrower range of services on a smaller scale. During the 70 years covered by the probate inventories there is evidence of only two blacksmiths, two carpenters, one bricklayer, one cordwainer, one weaver and one tailor. This range of crafts was just enough to service the basic needs of the village community. For other goods and services they could travel to the nearby markets in Rochester or Chatham.

Despite the rapid urban growth of the 17th and early 18th centuries, most land was still used for agriculture. Within the parish boundaries of Rochester, Chatham and Strood there were around 7,000 acres of farmland. The size of individual land-holdings varied considerably throughout the area, with a focus on arable farming with some livestock.[26]

In Gillingham three distinct groups relied on farming for an income: yeomen, husbandmen and those who combined another occupation with working a smallholding. The yeomen were the wealthiest group. Anthony Woodgate was typical, leaving goods valued at £383, the bulk of which was agricultural produce. His three barns contained wheat, oats, barley, beans, clover and peas as well as 40 acres of wheat 'on the ground'. He also owned cows, horses, sheep and pigs and all the farming equipment necessary to exploit his land. The husbandmen were less wealthy and cultivated a narrower range of crops. For example, Stephen Simons, with goods worth £53 in total at his death, had only six hogs and some wheat, barley and peas.[27]

There were many who combined work as craftsmen or employment in Chatham Dockyard with working a smallholding, providing a partial solution to the problem of delayed dockyard wages. There was a wide range of variation in the assets of this group and in the kinds of crops and livestock they owned. Some, like the labourer Richard Hunt who owned a couple of pigs, were safeguarding their food supply. At the other extreme, wealthy craftsmen like the shipwright William Mitchell owned five pigs, eight cows, eight acres of wheat in the field and a barn packed with barley, peas and hay.[28]

Housing

The hearth tax returns for the Medway area indicate that the more urban parishes had the highest proportion of larger houses, with around one in five dwellings having five or more hearths. In the more rural Gillingham, only one in 10 boasted this number. In all four communities most houses had only one or two hearths. It is perhaps indicative of the pressure on housing in Chatham caused by the rapid expansion of the dockyard workforce that not a single dwelling in that town is listed as empty, whereas all the other communities contain empty houses.[29]

The most common type of dwelling in all four communities was a two-up, two-down house. The ground-floor rooms were usually the kitchen and a living room, known as a 'hall' or 'parlour', although the former term was used less frequently in the 18th century. The two upstairs rooms, the chambers, often contained the most valuable items. As well as a bed and its mattress and hangings, the chambers could also contain household linen and furniture such as chairs, tables and cabinets. Many houses had another room in the roof, the 'garret', and a lean-to wash- or brew-house on the back and sometimes a cellar beneath. The way in which rooms were used differed slightly according to the occupation of the householder. In the home of an artisan a front room downstairs often served as a workshop and the room above was used to store materials and tools. Those who farmed often used this 'hall chamber' as a storage place for grain or other produce.

The contents of the larger houses suggest a comfortable lifestyle. When John King, a Gillingham yeoman, died in 1715, his substantial farmhouse was listed as having a kitchen and parlour, five chambers, a milk cellar, beer cellar and a brew-house. The kitchen was well stocked with utensils, tables and chairs and a clock. The parlour contained a feather bed, bolster and pillows, a couch, a dozen leather chairs and two round tables. Luxury items were also kept in the parlour: a punch bowl, pictures and a looking glass. Of the five chambers, the one over the kitchen held goods of the highest value. Two beds and their accessories, two chests of drawers, two tables, eight chairs, fire irons and bellows and household linen. The other four were rather more modestly furnished. One held a few bits of furniture, another two beds, and 'the maids Chamber' had a bed, a chest of drawers and a chest. Finally, 'the old chamber over the parlour' held nothing more than 'one sack of old seed &c worth £2 6s'. King's goods were valued at £617 9s. The shopkeeper Anne Foote enjoyed the luxury of a kitchen and a parlour as well as the shop on the ground floor of her house, with four chambers upstairs. She too owned luxury items – a clock and a looking glass were kept in her 'second best chamber'. Only two houses contained books. A widow, Crisogen Edridge, left two books and in the study of the vicar Ralph Twisse there were 'books as many as are valued at xi s'.[30]

Debt and Lending

The level of debt experienced by dockyard workers is evident in the inventories. Money due to dockyard workers could be a considerable portion of their estate. When John Haywood, a carpenter, died, his possessions were valued at £6 10s. and 'Money due to him for work in the King's Dock at Chatham, £46 13s 6d'. Richard Owen was owed £30 'for his service performed as a gunner at Hoo Ness fort'; this accounted for over three quarters of his recorded wealth. The government debt could be passed from the deceased to his family. When the widow Jane Sutton died in

1688 she still had not received the £36 11s. wages that had been outstanding at the time of her husband's death. Delays in receiving wages meant that many of the inhabitants of the Medway area ran into debt and almost half the inventories for Rochester and Chatham and a quarter of those for Gillingham show outstanding debts. As was often the case in rural communities in early modern England, women in Gillingham were prominent among the money lenders; five widows and a 'singlewoman' died with significant debts owing to them.[31]

This period in the history of the Medway Towns marked a turning point in the balance of power in the four communities. Chatham's victory over Rochester in securing the right to hold its own market was the first step in a struggle for equal status that would continue for the next two hundred years. Although Rochester enjoyed the more sophisticated political structure, the Chatham vestry shared its interests with a powerful ally, the Royal Navy. This, combined with a population that soon outstripped that of the ancient cathedral city, meant that Rochester's economic and political dominance was now threatened.

This jostling for position was evident in the built environment. Rochester re-emphasised its ancient traditions and judicial functions with the construction of fine new civic buildings. Chatham Dockyard continued to expand to meet the demands of international wars and, alongside fine warships, elegant naval buildings were constructed in brick, bringing a new air of permanence to this settlement. Around the dockyard the town of Chatham continued to grow and on the hill to the east of the dockyard buildings a new community called Brompton began to put down roots, signalling the beginning of Gillingham's transformation from a rural to an urbanised community and its absorption into the Medway complex.

constant succession
trade, hurry,
d business, upon
is river'

ward Hasted (1776)

During the mid-18th century visitors to the Medway area found themselves caught up in the hustle and bustle of what was fast becoming an urban sprawl with much new building to accommodate a steadily growing population. Most were dazzled by Rochester Bridge and the wonders of Chatham Dockyard, but not the middle-aged spinster Gertrude Savile. Arriving in the Medway area in the autumn of 1756 on an excursion from London, she grumbled her way through her stay. She spent the first night in Rochester at the *Black Bull* inn, 'tollerably civill treatment but intollerably dear. 'Tis a very old and ugly Town; did not see one brave street or good house in it. Pretty large, lies low upon the river Medway, which being at low water when I saw it, seem'd a poor little one.' After a bumpy carriage ride to Maidstone she returned to Chatham, which she dismissed with the terse comment: 'Looks like what it is – a seafaring, Tarlike Town.'[1]

For others, the Medway Towns was a place of opportunity. In the spring of 1759 the 19-year-old Mary Lacy escaped the drudgery of rural domestic service in the village of Ash near Canterbury. She stole men's clothes from her employer and travelled to Chatham. Arriving in the busy seafaring town she called herself William Chandler and soon found a place as apprentice to a ship's carpenter. Fifteen years later a 12-year-old Horatio Nelson arrived at Chatham after a six-hour coach journey from London, eager to join his first ship. He was to serve as midshipman on the *Raissonable*, but he

Figure 50 'The prospect of Chatham', 1738, showing the new housing development of Brompton on the hill and the extent of the dockyard buildings stretching from its northern wall on the left to St Mary's church and Chatham Quay on the right.

Figure 51 Captain Horatio Nelson (1758-1805) shown here in his early twenties, wearing his captain's uniform.

found no one to welcome him to the Medway. The captain, his uncle, was away on shore leave and had made no arrangements for the boy to be met. The young Nelson survived this first test of his mettle unscathed and successfully made his own way to the ship moored out on the river.[2]

Riverside society also offered social opportunities. In 1740 the historian Hasted's widowed mother moved to Chatham, leasing Rome House, an early 17th-century mansion on the outskirts of the town. According to Hasted, who was eight years old at the time and attended King's School in Rochester, his mother was 'young … cheerful and sprightly' and 'pleased with the gay round of company' offered by the Medway Towns.

Here they lived with great comfort and credit, visiting and being visited by all the Gentry of Rank and fortune, by the Commissioner's family, and by those of all the principal officers of the dockyard and of the army and navy quartered in both Rochester and Chatham.[3]

THE EXPANDING TOWNSCAPE

The open fields that had existed between Rochester and Chatham disappeared as the population of Chatham grew steadily from around 5,000 in 1720 to 6,000 in the 1780s. Gertrude Savile observed the ribbon development, noting that there was 'no intermission or space between the Houses nor paved way. From the hills about it, it seems one long street only.'[4]

Brompton

There was still open farmland between Chatham and the village of Gillingham, but that was slowly being built upon. The development of Brompton (now known as Old Brompton) began in the second half of the 17th century. The growth of this new community in the parish of Gillingham was prompted by Chatham Dockyard expanding northwards along the riverbank from its original site

Figure 52 Brompton village in the parish of Gillingham, adjacent to the boundary with the parish of Chatham and overlooking the dockyards and the river.

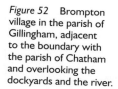

Figure 53 Prospect Row was was built in stages. Many of the smart two-storey houses built in the late 17th and early 18th centuries were raised and rewindowed later, and some were completely replaced, creating an irregular, picturesque effect.

on Gun Wharf. The village grew on flat ground at the crest of a hill overlooking the dockyards and the Medway, where the land fell away steeply to the west towards the river and more gently eastwards towards the village of Gillingham. The new settlement grew quickly and was soon characterised by terraced housing on streets laid out in a regular grid pattern.

The occupants of Brompton in the 18th century ranged from the more prosperous dockyard officials and naval officers to the lowlier dockyard workers. A large number of inns and lodging houses catered for seamen discharged from ships undergoing repairs. Richard Ruffel, gunner on Mary Lacy's first ship, 'lived in lodgings in a place called Brompton, near Chatham'. From the mid-18th century the area was also used for soldiers and sailors of the Marine Corps who, as yet, had no barracks.[5]

Among the earliest surviving buildings in Brompton are the houses in Prospect Row. As the name suggests, when these were first built the inhabitants had a fine view over the river Medway. The first building at the north end of the row, now the *King George V* pub, is thought to be the oldest building in Brompton and dates from 1685. The earliest buildings in the terraced row have two storeys and steeply pitched roofs while the later, 18th-century, buildings have three storeys and a parapet.

Figure 54 House on the corner of Prospect row, Brompton, perhaps the first in the row and thought to date from 1685. It was altered with new windows in the 19th century and later converted into a public house called the *George V*. The neighbouring houses, with coloured brickwork and fine timber doorcases and cornices, have kept the original character of the earliest houses here.

CHANGES IN CHATHAM DOCKYARD

The role of Chatham Dockyard

During the course of the 18th century the main function of Chatham Dockyard changed. From being an operational yard which offered a home for the British naval fleet, as it had been in the 16th and 17th centuries, it became a yard primarily for the building and repairing of ships. There were two reasons for this.

Ethnic Minorities in the Medway Towns

From the 17th century onwards there is evidence in local records of the presence of people from ethnic minorities in the Medway Towns. Much research still remains to be done but it is clear that the area, in common with other ports and dockyard towns, saw a range of different ethnic and national groups. Some merely passed through but others settled and became part of a diverse local community. One group for whom research has begun is black people of African, American and Caribbean origin.

The parish register for Strood records the christening of a 'black man' in 1655, and the burial of 'a seaman, negro' is recorded in the register for Chatham in 1659. By the 18th century entries in the registers reflect the fashion for black servants and slaves, for example the Gillingham register for 1763 records the baptism of George St George, 'a negro boy belonging to Mr Cherry'. Other records suggest permanent residence. The members of the Rochester Bethel Methodist church in 1784 included James Filley and John Sharp, both described as 'negro', and a history of the church refers to two black women employed as chapel keepers.

One man that settled was Chatham Cuffay, who came to the Medway from St Kitts. The first mention of him in the records is when, aged 17 in 1772, he was christened in St Mary's church, Chatham. Fourteen years later he married Juliana Fox, a local woman, at Gillingham parish church and they remained in the area and had five children. Their eldest son, William Cuffay, was apprenticed to a Chatham tailor but moved to London as a young man and became a prominent member of the Chartist movement. Arrested for his political activities, he was transported to Tasmania in 1848 where he remained until his death in 1870.

By the second half of the 19th century black people are found in all walks of life in the Medway Towns. Both the Church of England and nonconformists welcomed

Figure B   *William Cuffay, born in Chatham in 1788, son of Chatham Cuffay who moved from St Kitts to the Medway.*

visiting black preachers, the music halls and theatres starred black entertainers and there were black workers in local industries such as the dockyards and brickfields. Joshua Campbelton was one of these. Born in 1820 in Bermuda or North America (there is conflicting census evidence), he served in the Royal Navy for over 20 years. He married Harriet, a Chatham woman, in 1851. By 1864 Joshua had left the navy and was working as a labourer in Chatham Dockyard. While working on the *Achilles*, the first iron battleship to be built at the yard, an accident caused the death of a fellow worker and Joshua lost a leg. Despite his disability he continued to work in the dockyard for at least the next 10 years. After several unsuccessful applications he was finally admitted to the Sir John Hawkins Hospital, where he remained until his death in 1902.

Date of Applica-tion.	Name and Address of Applicant	Last rating.	Age last Birthday.	Age of Wife (if any).	Number of chil-dren de-pendent.	Number of years Servitude.		Character as shewn on Certificates.	Pension	Income from any other source.
						Afloat.	Harbour.			
1872 Aug 6	Joshua Campbelton 2 George Street Fair Row Chatham	Ship's Cook	54	44	5	21 years	—	7 good 9 very good	£30..8.0	Labour in Dock Yard as Wpt bricklr. lost a Dock Ya
1875 Aug 6	John H. Ogborn 3 Camperdown Cottage Burnt Oak Gillingham	Able Seamen	51	42	—	12 years	2 years	good	£11.0.0	none lost a leg on July 1. the Dockyd 4 January 1864
1875 Aug 6	Thomas John Harris 6 Victoria Street	Gunners Mr.	56	60	1	20 years	14 years	very good	£25.—.	Labourer in Check Yard

Figure A   *An extract from the records of the Sir John Hawkins Hospital for 1875 showing his, on this occasion, unsuccessful application for entry from Joshua Campbelton. His is the top entry and gives details of his naval service, his income and his accident in the dockyard.*

Sources: Much of this panel is based on material researched by volunteers Brian Joyce and Sandra Fowler. Additional material has come from B. Joyce, *Black People in Medway 1655-1914* (Rochester 2010), which offers considerable detail on the topic of black people in the Medway Towns. See also B. Aubry, *William Cuffay – Medway's Black Chartist* (Rochester 2008).

Figure 55 The *Victory* sailing from Spithead, painted by Robert Dodd, 1791. She was a First Rate ship, with a crew of over 800 and 104 guns. Of the 27 battleships that fought at Trafalgar, only three, including *Victory*, were First Rates.

First, the changing international focus of British foreign policy, trade and exploration meant that Portsmouth and Plymouth offered harbours and dockyards that were more strategically placed for conflict and trade in the Atlantic. Second, the river Medway presented problems for the 18th-century naval fleet. Although never easy to navigate, the Medway had been ideal for the 17th-century fleet which spent half the year in port, but by the 18th century the navy was expected to be ready to depart at any moment. Awkward currents made exit and entry to the Medway a slow and unpredictable business and contributed to the decline in Chatham's use as an operational naval base. The situation was summed up by the Earl of Sandwich in his 1773 report to the Admiralty on the future of Chatham Dockyard. In his view:

> if it is kept singly to its proper use as a building yard possibly more useful service may be obtained from it than any other dockyard in His Majesties dominions; the great extent of the yard which faces the river and the great length of the harbour which has room to moor half the fleet of England of a moderate draught of water are conveniences that are not to be found elsewhere; ... the best use to be made of this port now, is to build or repair ships sent from Portsmouth or Plymouth therefore all improvements at this yard should be for that end, in preference to any other considerations, only smaller ships should be laid up constantly here.[6]

It was in Chatham Dockyard that Nelson's flagship, the *Victory*, was built. The order to build a new First Rate warship of 100 guns was received in Chatham in July 1759 and she took seven years to build at a cost of £63,176 (the equivalent today of the cost of an aircraft carrier) and then was laid up until she became Admiral Keppel's flagship in 1778. She sailed as the flagship of 12 other admirals until she came under the command of Admiral Nelson in 1803.[7]

Building in Chatham Dockyard

Although the role of Chatham Dockyard changed during the 18th century, the infrastructure to support the naval function continued to expand and the spectacle continued to impress. Writing in the 1770s, Charles Seymour observed:

> Here are whole streets of Warehouses and Storehouses. This celebrated Dock-yard, including the Ordnance Wharf, is about one mile in length … and is adorned with many elegant buildings, inhabited by the Commissioner, and principal officers belonging to the yard, which bespeak the opulence of the nation and the importance of the Navy. Here are many neat and commodious Offices, for transacting the business of the Yards, also immense Store-houses, and work rooms.[8]

The 1720s in Chatham Dockyard saw the completion of the building programme that had begun earlier in the century. A handsome terrace of 12 houses was constructed to house the officers of the yard and the wall encircling the docks was finished. Also, outside the yard, on the riverside crossing over into

Figure 56 The Officers' Terrace, Chatham Dockyard, built in 1722-31 and probably designed by the Navy Board. It is the finest of such terraces to survive in a navy yard. Each house was allotted to an officer of the dockyard, who conducted his business from the basement, and each had a rear service wing and yard as well as stabling and a walled garden on the far side of a back lane.

Rochester, the navy's victualling yard continued to expand with the building of new storehouses. Adjacent to the dockyard, between St Mary's church and the river, the Ordnance Board added sheds, cranes and a house for the master gunner to the Gun Wharf. According to Hasted, the ammunition and weaponry for use by the navy was an impressive sight.

> The guns belonging to the royal shipping in this river are deposited on this wharf in long tiers, and large pyramids of canon-balls are laid up on it, ready for service; there is likewise a continued range of storehouses ... in one of them is a small armoury of muskets, pistols, cutlasses and pikes, poleaxes, and other hostile weapons arranged in proper order.[9]

Fluctuations in the workforce

International relations also had an impact on the local workforce. Britain was at peace between the end of the Jacobite uprisings in 1719 and the outbreak of war with Spain in 1739. As a consequence the demand for new warships fell and Chatham endured two decades of recession. Dockyard employment, the mainstay of the town's economy, fell from 1,175 in 1710 to 793 by 1725 and the number employed in the ropeyard was halved, falling from 136 to 70 in the same period. Employment continued at a reduced level throughout the 1720s and only began to rise again in the late 1730s with the outbreak of the War of Jenkin's Ear with Spain. In 1738 there were 1,300 employees and this rose to 1,700 by 1742. For the rest of the century levels of employment in the yards remained steady, never falling below 1,600 even in peacetime, and rising to above two thousand in 1799.[10]

Disputes in Chatham Dockyard

The better organisation of disputes that began to emerge in the 18th century reflected changes in the workforce at Chatham. In the 16th and 17th centuries employment had been irregular and fluctuations in personnel and in levels of employment limited the men's bargaining power with the Navy Board. By the middle decades of the 18th century demand for ships was steadier and on a more permanent basis. Instead of an itinerant workforce the yard employed those who had put down roots in the local community. Negotiations with the Navy Board in the 1739 strike were conducted by men who were Chatham householders or freemen of Rochester. Although better organised, strikes achieved only limited success.[11]

From the late 17th century disputes in Chatham Dockyard were related to working practices and the matter of 'chips', a perk in the form of pieces of timber traditionally granted to dockyard workers. On 28 August 1739 220 shipwrights at Chatham went on strike because some of their fellow workers had been fined and dismissed for laziness. The following day, the shipwrights' apprentices marched through Rochester in protest and strikers gathered at the dockyard gate to stop anyone from entering or leaving. As the day wore on, the men became drunk and Commissioner Matthews reported to the Navy Board that some 'behaved with all the insolence imaginable'. A justice of the peace read the Riot Act, but with little effect.

When Matthews appealed to the Navy Board in London for help, he was told to meet workers' demands. The navy's priority was to have the fleet ready for the recently declared war with Spain. Four members of the Board went to Chatham on 30 August and after discussions with the workforce and the officers in charge of the yard it was agreed that the fines and dismissals were unjustified and that the privilege of 'chips' should be reinstated. The men returned to work on 1 September but the authorities did not forget the strike action. Within three weeks the ringleaders had been dismissed.[12]

The rope makers went on strike in 1745 to protest against what they saw as the over-recruitment of apprentices to meet the demands of war. They attempted to get support for their action from rope makers in other naval dockyards but none was forthcoming and the Navy Board was not in a mood to negotiate. The ringleaders were arrested immediately and the men told to return to work or face dismissal.

In 1756 a dispute over the dockyard workers' right to 'chips' brought the shipwrights out on strike again. The Navy Board's attempt to curb the abuse of this perk by enforcing the rule that each man could only take what he could carry under one arm was met with defiance. Shipwrights gathered outside the Commissioner's house in protest and when they refused to return to work the gates of Chatham Dockyard were closed. The workers broke down the gates and called a strike. The stoppage was well supported but the Navy Board made it clear that they were ready to sack those who continued to strike. Within a week the men returned to work and carried their 'chips' home under their arm.[13]

Towards the end of the century the shipwrights resisted changes in working practice. The strike of 1775 was prompted by the Navy Board's decision to introduce 'task work' or piece work, with the idea of increasing productivity. The practice was introduced at Chatham as an experiment. The shipwrights contacted their fellow workers at Plymouth and Portsmouth and they planned joint strike action. They petitioned the Navy Board, claiming that task work 'added oppression to distress, and made them more miserable and wretched still'. A strike began in Chatham on 5 July and early offers of concessions by the Navy Board were rejected outright by the shipwrights. The board responded by dismissing all of the 400 striking shipwrights. Five weeks later the shipwrights returned to work but the ringleaders were not re-employed. In 1782 the Earl of Sandwich reported that the men of Chatham yard had 'been brought to adopt this plan and are now eager in the execution of it'.[14]

The military presence

Although Chatham was no longer home to the British fleet, the importance of Chatham Dockyard to naval strategy led to improved defences and an increased military presence in the town during the course of the 18th century.

The Chatham Lines

Building work began with the construction of the Chatham Lines, sited on the high ground to the east of Chatham Dockyard. This fortification was built to defend the dockyard from an attack from the land and to protect the main road to London. The project had been conceived following the Dutch attack on the Medway in 1667. Land was purchased in 1708-9 but work did not begin until the 1750s, prompted by the threat of invasion posed by the Seven Years' War. Between 1755 and 1758 a series of ramparts and ditches were built, starting east of Gun Wharf, encircling Chatham

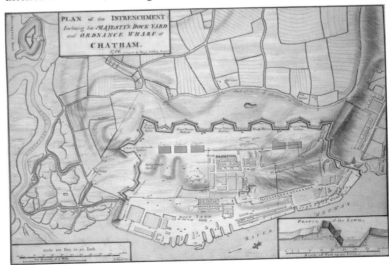

Figure 57 The plan for the first stage of the defences known as the Chatham Lines, drawn up in 1756. The fortifications were designed to protect the dockyard from a landward attack. Between 1755 and 1758 ramparts and ditches were built which completely surrounded Chatham Dockyard and Brompton village.

PLAN of the INTRENCHMENT Including his MAJESTY'S DOCK YARD and ORDNANCE WHARF at CHATHAM.

Figure 58 Chatham Barracks, built in 1760. The layout of the barrack blocks was as they are shown in the previous illustration.

Dockyard and Brompton village and ending at the river to the north-west of the dockyard.

Fifteen years later the Lines were extended to the north as far as St Mary's Creek, plans were made to extend fortifications eastwards towards Rochester and a redoubt was added that would become known as Fort Amherst. The flat open land around the fortifications was referred to as the 'field of fire', an area which gave no shelter to an approaching enemy.

With improved fortifications came an increased number of soldiers and marines in the area. The 1750s saw the first permanent accommodation for the armed forces in the Medway Towns. Chatham Barracks was built inside the Lines and was ready to receive its first infantry regiment in 1760. Twenty years later barracks were also built on Dock Road to house 600 marines of the Chatham Division.[15]

ECONOMIC LIFE ON THE RIVER

Figure 59 Apprenticeship registration by trade 1750-69.

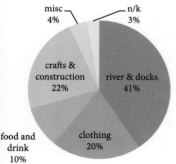

The records of apprenticeships registered in the Guildhall at Rochester in the latter half of the 18th century show how important the river was to the local economy. These records hold details of the masters recruiting in the area and the apprentices they took on. Of the 316 apprentices registered in the period 1750-69, 41 per cent entered trades related to the river. Of this group, about half entered land-based specialist trades related to shipbuilding and fitting: most in the sector became shipwrights and the rest entered specialised trades including caulking and sail, rope, oar and block making. The other half of the river-based apprentices went to sea as fishermen and dredgermen or mariners. The expansion of the towns is evident from the 22 per cent of boys apprenticed to craftsmen and construction trades; house carpenters and glaziers, brickmakers and ironmongers were recruited steadily throughout the period. Also important were those who provided the necessities of life for the population of the Medway Towns. The tailors, cordwainers and perrukemakers ensured that people were clothed, shod and be-wigged, while the food and drink industries fed and watered the inhabitants.[16]

Fishing and oyster dredging

The management of fishing

All fishing on the Medway continued to be controlled by the Admiralty Court. Concern that the ancient traditions and rules for fishing and dredging the river were being flouted led to the 1728 Act of Parliament for 'regulating, well ordering, governing and improving the Oyster Fishery in the river Medway and waters thereof, under the authority of the Mayor and Citizens of the City of Rochester'. The regulations controlled the timing and location of dredging, for preserving stocks and for 'setting the stint', the amount of catch that each dredgerman could take from the oyster beds. All fishermen were jointly liable for the costs of the administration of the fishing grounds and the expenses of the Admiralty Court, each paying 6s. 8d. every year. Unfortunately this did not prove to be enough. By 1865 the Oyster Fishery was £20,000 in the red and a new Act was needed to free the oyster dredgers from their communal debt.[17]

The fishermen of Strood

Most fishermen lived in Rochester and Strood. Masters in those two communities registered similar numbers of apprentices. However, Strood, a village of a few hundred inhabitants, relied far more heavily on fishing for a living than did Rochester, with a population of several thousand. Nearly half of all apprentices came from Strood. Samuel Ireland observed that 'In the town of Strood little occurs worth recording' but went on to acknowledge the community was 'principally supported by the oyster fishery'.[18]

Fishing and dredging on the Medway could be a profitable business and many of the oyster fishers and dredgers owned several boats. James Humphrey, a fisherman of Strood who died in 1727, was typical. His probate inventory records that he lived in a sizeable house with three bed-chambers and a garret above a large ground-floor room and that he also owned a separate warehouse and storehouse. The detailed list of fishing equipment includes three sailing vessels: 'the great smack', 'a stoe boat' and 'a new boat'.[19]

Figure 60 Quarry Farm, Frindsbury, one of the places where cargoes were unloaded to avoid paying dues at the Rochester Quays. The red brick Quarry House, shown in the foreground, was built in the 17th century and demolished in the late 19th century.

Shipbuilding and river trade

Rochester, like Chatham, was largely reliant on the river and Chatham Dockyard for its continuing prosperity. In Hasted's description of the town he noted that 'the intercourse of the inhabitants with the Royal Dock, Victualling Office, Navy and other branches of the shipping prove a continual source of wealth and employment to them … and though there are no particular manufactures carried on here, makes it a very populous and busy town'. Shipbuilding also took place on the Rochester riverside. Another contemporary, Charles Seymour, mentioned that 'Exclusive of the royal dock-yard, at Chatham, there are several private yards for building ships; in one of them several men of war have been built.' This is probably a reference to Thomas Seward's yard in Rochester where the *Maidstone*, a 28-gun warship, was launched in 1748. There were also private shipyards across the river in Frindsbury.[20]

Much of Rochester's income was from river trade. By the mid-18th century, around half of all shipping from Kentish ports went in and out of the Rochester quays and it was reported in 1776 that 'Near 200 sail arrive annually in the port'. It was very much a two-way traffic. The main imports were coal, malt and barley to support the rapidly growing brewing industries in Chatham and Maidstone. Other imports, largely for domestic consumption, were groceries, wine and tobacco. Exported goods included fuller's earth, used in cloth-making, oysters and wool. The main agricultural export was oats, most of which went to London.[21]

Much of the river traffic and the goods it transported were from or destined for Maidstone and other towns further upriver. The Medway was navigable as far as Maidstone and Tonbridge, although Rochester bridge presented a problem to larger vessels. Ships bringing goods for transport upriver had to stop at Rochester's quays, just below the bridge, and transfer their load to smaller boats. Barges were able to pass under the bridge but they often caused damage. In 1798 Daniel Alexander, the bridge architect, complained that they caused considerable 'delays, inconveniences and accidents'. One way for ships to avoid both this problem and also to dodge the port dues at Rochester was to load and unload away from the town quays in the many creeks below the bridge, much to the annoyance of the port authority. For example, in 1737 the Bridgewardens complained that the wharf near Quarry Farm in Frindsbury was used for the informal traffic of corn and timber.[22]

Copperas

A more unusual river-related activity was the copperas production, sited to the north of the parish of Gillingham on

Dredging for oysters

Oyster dredging was a wet, cold and demanding activity carried out in the waters of the Medway estuary area for centuries under the control of the Rochester Oyster Fishery. On the river Medway the traditional vessel used for dredging was the bawley boat. Similar to the 'smacks' used for oyster dredging elsewhere on the Kent coast, the bawley boats were small and light, about 12 yards long with a displacement of 15-20 tons. Bawleys were half-decked and had a wet well to keep the catch alive. Each bawley would drag five to six dredges.

The dredges used to gather the oysters from the sea bed were triangular in shape, and made of wrought iron with 'rigging' attached. They were hooked onto the boat, cast into the sea and pulled through the oyster beds. The dredge scraped along the bottom of the beds

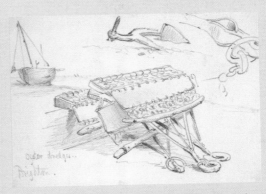

Figure B   *An oyster dredge, dragged along the riverbed from the bawley boat to collect the shellfish.*

lifting the oysters into its mesh. Casting out the dredges was a skilled task, if too much rope were let out the dredge would bite deep into the bed, if too little then it would only pick up loose stones or shells. The dredges, which weighed perhaps a half-hundredweight when full, were hauled on to deck and emptied before being cast out again. Their contents were examined and sorted – the catch was sorted into baskets and rinsed ready for market – the unwanted rubble comprising shells, shingle and immature or damaged oysters was swept back into the sea.

Dredging oysters for sale was seasonal work, carried out between October and April. In the closed season from May to September, when the oysters were spawning, boats and equipment were overhauled and the oyster beds were cultivated. Samples were taken and tested, predators such as starfish, sting winkles or whelks were sifted out and destroyed, and young oysters were caught and transferred to places where they would thrive.

Today the Rochester Oyster Fishery still holds the annual Admiralty Court at the beginning of July, presided over by the mayor of Rochester, and it continues to regulate fishing on the River Medway and on its creeks and tributaries between Garrison Point, Sheerness and Hawkwood Stone.

Figure A   *A bawley boat moored on the river at Strood, with Rochester bridge and castle in the background.*

Further Reading:
D. Coombe, *The Bawleymen* (1979)
R. Goodsall, 'Oyster fisheries on the north Kent coast', *Archaeologica Cantiana*, LXXX (1965).

Thanks are due to Jane Bryan-Brown for her help in researching this topic.

what is now Copper House Marsh. The Gillingham works was the smallest producer in Kent, overshadowed by those at Whitstable and Queenborough on the coast and by Deptford, Greenwich and Rotherhithe on the banks of the Thames. Copperas stones, consisting of iron pyrites, were collected from the riverbed and placed in water-covered 'beds' on land where they were left for up to six years. The resulting liquid was boiled down to produce ferrous sulphate crystals and then moulded into cakes for transportation. The main use for the resulting 'green vitriol' was as a dye fixative for woollens. It was also used as an element in printer's ink, a tanning agent for leather and in gunpowder manufacture.[23]

In the 1760s the Gillingham works, owned by William Truin of Rochester, produced around 120 tons of copperas a year. The copperas works themselves would have operated with a workforce of around ten men with added employment for villagers gathering the copperas stones from the riverbed at low tide. A report of 1584 on the Kent industry noted that 'the stuffe is gathered by poore men women and children inhabitants hereabouts'. The report suggested that children aged 10 could collect around four bushels of stones in a tide, which would have weighed around 680lbs, and adults two to three times that amount. This hard labour was claimed to have given 'good reliefe to their comforte and contentment.'[24]

Brewing

Brewing was an important and steadily growing industry in the Medway Towns. Beer was needed not only for the local population but also to supply ships. The naval victualling yards at Chatham looked to local brewers to meet the peaks and troughs of demand generated by the mobilisation of the royal naval fleet.[25]

There were many small breweries in the area but by far the largest and most profitable was Best's brewery. The family had obtained a contract to supply the Navy in the 17th century and continued to profit from this opportunity for 200 years. The company's profits were at their peak in the mid-18th century under the under the management of fourth-generation brewer James Best.[26]

The naval contract helped to secure the family's fortunes and they capitalised on this by making astute marriages. James' grandfather Thomas married Elizabeth Mawdistley, the heiress to another wealthy local brewing family, and his aunt married Admiral Vernon, thus strengthening the naval connection.

The family also established a strong political profile in the local community. Best men were members of the Chatham vestry in the 1660s and took a lead in Chatham's resistance to Rochester's attempt to suppress Chatham market. James and his father Mawdistley both served as High Sheriff for Kent, and Mawdistley also purchased Park House at Boxley in 1720, signalling his family's rising prestige by establishing a home on a country estate.[27]

James' business success was also due to his willingness to take on new ideas and adapt practices. He almost doubled the company's production of beer from around 11,000 barrels in 1744 to over 23,000 in 1772 and supplied beer throughout the Medway area. Although the Navy remained his largest customer, 95 public houses, nearly half of which were in Chatham, supplied Best beer to thirsty sailors and dockyard workers. Best also began to accumulate tied public houses. In 1743 there were only three houses tied to Best Brewery but the number had increased to 27 by 1787. The company's property holdings also increased as the business premises on the Chatham wharves expanded and additional land and property was purchased in the area.[28]

James enjoyed his wealth. He built himself a prestigious new home, known as Chatham House, and furnished it extravagantly, spending over £1,000 on furniture and wallpaper. When he married he spent the same amount on jewellery for his wife and his accounts suggest that his personal expenses continued to grow as his family increased. They went on trips to France and his sons were educated at Eton and travelled abroad. When James died in 1782 his business was inherited jointly by his three sons. They did not approach the business with the same energy and interest as their father and profits slumped. The business remained in the family until 1851 when it was sold to another local brewery, Messrs Winch.[29]

POLITICAL DIFFERENCES

Chatham had no MP of its own and was reliant on the county MP for representation in Parliament. Local administration continued under the authority of the church vestry. By contrast, Rochester had its ancient charter, mayor and town hall and the luxury of electing two MPs. The relationship between the aldermen of Rochester and the parish vestry in Chatham continued to be an uneasy one throughout the 18th century and Chatham remained at a political disadvantage.

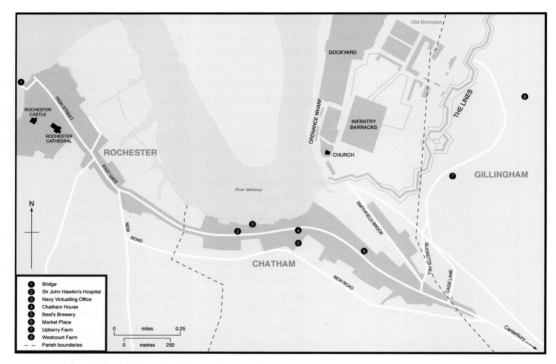

Figure 61 Map showing the proposed new road which bypassed Chatham High Street and the position of the Chatham Lines. Also marked is the position of the Navy Victualling Office (3), Chatham House, the home of James Best (4) and Best's Brewery (5).

Conflict of interest over the roads

Towards the end of the century the continuing rivalry between Chatham and Rochester was evident in the tussle over improving the roads in the two communities. In 1769 the Rochester corporation invited Chatham and Strood to join forces with them in obtaining a bill to improve the streets and also to build a new road that would avoid the congestion of central Chatham. After discussion between Rochester corporation and the Chatham vestry, the latter 'Resolved unanimously not to join with them or be concerned in the said bill'. They believed that the changes would bring economic disadvantage by diverting traffic on the London to Dover road away from Chatham High Street. Rochester and Strood went ahead with improvements to the existing streets. Hasted commented that Strood was 'much improved of late years' by this act for paving and lighting, the cost of which was partially subsidised by income from the toll-gate.[30]

Rochester's improvements brought disadvantage to Chatham. They acknowledged that 'if the town of Chatham too was not made more safe and commodious for travellers, the greater part of them would probably avoid so unsafe and disagreeable a thoroughfare by travelling the new road'. In 1772 the Chatham vestry obtained their own paving and lighting act to improve the 'narrow thoroughfare so disagreeable to passengers'.[31]

A clause in Chatham's act which referred to 'every part of the High Street of Chatham' in 'places contiguous to this town' caused Rochester to oppose the act, fearing that the Chatham vestry would gain authority in the parts of Rochester that bordered Chatham. Their fears were allayed by the insertion of a clause which said that 'Nothing in this Act shall in any matter lessen or effect the jurisdiction of the said city of Rochester'.[32]

The rivalry between the two communities did not prevent them from joining forces when it suited them. Disputes with the national authorities over the expansion of Chatham Dockyard and the building of accommodation for the armed forces brought them together. In 1758 the vestry minutes of the parish of St Mary's, Chatham, record their displeasure at the loss of parish rights over the land on which the new garrison and Chatham Barracks had been built. Six men were chosen by the vestry to put their case to the Ordnance Board for the 'rights and privileges ... that they have been deprived of by the government building a Garrison'. The following year parishioners from Chatham and Rochester petitioned Parliament, objecting to the proposed enlargement of Chatham Dockyard. Neither complaint was upheld, although in 1786 the Ordnance Board did give some land back to the parish of St Mary's in Chatham for a burial ground.[33]

THE POOR

The 18th century brought changes to the way the poor were supported in the local community, with greater emphasis on 'indoor relief' rather than making payments to those in need. This was formalised by the Workhouse Test Act of 1723, which required that a person who wanted to receive poor relief had to enter a workhouse and work in return for their upkeep. Strood workhouse was built before the act was passed. It was part of a vanguard movement promoted by the Society for the Promotion of Christian Knowledge and was the first of its kind in Kent. The project was instigated by Caleb Parfect, vicar of Strood, and paid for out of the £60 per annum given for poor relief to the parish of Strood by the Watt's Charity of Rochester (see Ch 2). Parfect had high hopes for this new institution: 'This Workhouse will prove an happy expedient to bring all idle people to such an habit of industry, that there will not be a beggar bred in the Parish; nor can there be a miserable person in the nation, if the same course be taken through it.'

The Strood workhouse was built in the north-eastern corner of St Nicholas Churchyard, at a cost of £360. According to

Parfect the enterprise was both beneficial to the poor and economical for the parish. The orphans who were kept in the workhouse were employed in spinning for part of each day. 'These children us'd to be kept in poor families at 2/- per week but now they are inur'd to labour and help maintain themselves, earning at least their diet.' Attention was also paid to their future employment: girls were 'taught to knit their own stockings and to make their caps, aprons and shifts; to clean the House, make beds, to assist in washing and getting up the cloaths, dressing of victuals, and such other offices, as will make them good servants.' Parfect was also concerned to protect orphan boys from being apprenticed at too young an age. 'We now find Parish officers too eager to get rid of them; and they place them out so young, with little money ... to sorry masters, that 'tis little better than murdering them.'

Economies were also made in respect of the elderly and sick by forcing them to enter the workhouse to receive relief. The elderly and widows who were healthy said that they 'would drink less strong beer ... and work their fingers to the bone before they would come into the House'. Sick travellers had previously been lodged in a local inn, a practice which in Parfect's view was expensive and extravagant: 'many have pretended themselves sick for the sake of being sent to such quarters'. By insisting that the sick should enter the workhouse he claimed that 'we have not had half the trouble as before'.[34]

Although Strood led the way with this innovation in poor relief, the other Medway Towns soon followed suit once the Workhouse Test Act was passed. Two workhouses were erected in Rochester in 1724, one in each of the two parishes in the town, paid for by donations from the two local MPs, Sir

Figure 62 a) The workhouse in the parish of St Margaret's, Rochester, was built in 1724. It remained in use until 1859 when it became a national school. The attic still has its original sleeping cubicles. b) Inscription over the main doorway.

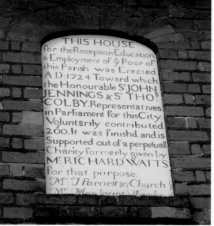

Thomas Colby and Sir John Jennings. The Rochester MPs also contributed £100 each to the voluntary subscription to raise the money needed to build Chatham workhouse. Although nearly £900 was collected, the vestry had to borrow to complete the building work and between 1725-7 an imposing three-storey building was erected at the east end of the High Street. The economic advantage of this method of providing for the poor was clear. The 1732 edition of *An Account of Several Work-houses for Employing and Maintaining the Poor* claimed that before the introduction of the workhouse the annual cost of poor relief in Chatham averaged £945, whereas the workhouse cost only £574 per year to care for 73 inmates. These inmates were kept occupied and contributed to their keep by picking oakum – unravelling tarred ropes – for use in the dockyard.[35]

Rochester, Chatham, Gillingham and Strood shared a common economic dependence on the river Medway but each retained a distinct identity throughout the middle years of the 18th century. Chatham was defined by the dockyard and the military presence, as was the new community known as Brompton in the parish of Gillingham. The west and south of the parish of Gillingham focused more on farming and fishing. Rochester maintained its gentility; Hasted described the cathedral city as a civilised and prosperous community:

> The buildings have been, of late years, much improved; in the streets are some commodious shops, and in several parts of the town many houses fit for the residence of small genteel families … Few places, at the distance of 30 miles from London, have a more frequent intercourse with the metropolis, carriages continually passing between Dover and London. The banks of the Medway are the rural and pleasant walks of this city. An assembly, a coffee house, and a circulating library, contribute to vary the amusements of this place … There are three capital and spacious inns … which vie with most in England for good accommodations.[36]

Strood, on the far side of Rochester bridge, was known primarily for its fishermen and oyster dredgers but was also notable among local people for an annual three-day fair in August at the feast of the Assumption, a privilege granted to the monks of Rochester by King John in 1206. The fair continued until the 1970s and the land near Strood railway station on which it was held still provides winter quarters for the Showman's Guild. Thomas Austin, vicar of the nearby parish of All Hallows, described the event in verse in 1756:

A fair there is just centr'd in a town,
More famed for ruder fishermen than clown;
Next to an open marsh the stalls are placed,
And with one double row of trifles graced.
Here come from *Roffa's* further streets, a throng
Of various maidens, beauties old and young,
Who having laid aside, for one small space,
Their darning, knitting, needlework and lace

Austin tells how the young women of Rochester (Roffa) met up
with the young men, then describes the opportunities offered by
the fair for shopping, gambling and eating the local delicacies:

But would you have the quintessence of all?
Then step you to the Oyster-wench's stall;
There crabs and shrimps (both stinking) new you'll buy,
Your palate teasing till you come to try.[37]

Chapter 6

War, Popular Protest and Fire, 1780-1820

Britain was at war with America from 1776 until 1783 and with France from 1793 to 1801 and from 1802 to 1815. These conflicts had a considerable impact on Chatham Dockyard and the Medway Towns. New warships were required and those damaged in naval battles needed to be repaired. The strategic importance of the dockyard placed the whole of the Medway area at risk of a French invasion. In response to this very real threat the military presence in the towns became all the more prominent and defences were strengthened. An increased naval and military significance brought new people to the towns, which in turn created a demand for new housing and new churches to accommodate them. In short, the Medway Towns became even more important to the nation at the end of the 18th century and this growth in importance was reflected in the expansion of the population and the urban environment.

Figure 63 Panorama of Strood, Rochester and Chatham, 1808, showing the continuous townscape along the banks of the Medway which had developed by that time, and the hilltop defences overlooking the towns. Fort Amherst and Fort Pitt are clearly visible.

Figure 64 A view of the
Medway estuary from the
hill above Strood in the
1790s, depicting the rural
setting of the riverside
communities.

When John Gale Jones visited the area in 1796, his observations
suggest that this expansion was not yet all-encompassing. He, like
most other visitors, recorded that Rochester and Chatham were
joined along the length of 'one continued street' but noted that
Gillingham was still 'a small village, some two miles distant from
Chatham'. In a chaise on his way to a meeting in the village of
Luton, a community that would become a working-class suburb
of Chatham during the course of the 19th century, he noted that
'the road through which I passed was very rugged. Several times I
expected to be overturned.'[1]

Reflecting the romantic mood of the times, Jones also recorded
the pastoral beauty of the area surrounding the industrial-military
complex. Returning from Luton he waxed lyrical on the 'beautiful
prospect' that greeted him on his journey to Chatham. 'The hills of
the surrounding county seemed to rear their proud, aspiring heads,
and the pure Medway, with its silver stream, gently meandered
through the verdant meads, and watered the fruitful valley.' Most
of the men that he met in these outlying areas were farmers and
millers. The local doctor in Gillingham who gave Jones a bed for
the night lived very modestly, 'as the neighbourhood, beside being
small, was so poor, as not to be able to afford being often ill'.[2]

Despite these rural surroundings, for the majority of the
inhabitants of the Medway communities, life was essentially urban
in character. As the towns grew, the balance between Rochester
and Chatham changed. John Gale Jones was the first commentator
to observe that the cathedral city was being overtaken by
neighbouring Chatham. He was not particularly impressed by
either, suggesting that the improvements to the roads, promised by
the acts of the 1770s and '90s, had only limited impact by 1796:

Rochester, although called a city, is yet far from deserving that denomination, either from its size or its respectability. It forms but one continued street, which is neither paved not lighted, and the inhabitants do not appear to abound in excessive opulence. Chatham, to which it immediately joins, and of which it seems but a part, is of the two the worst, being extremely dirty, and much occupied by soldiers.[3]

The increasing dominance of Chatham was also evident in Hasted's comment, made around the same time, that Rochester market was 'now almost deserted, the market of the adjoining town of Chatham supplying the place of it'.[4]

The community at Brompton, overlooking Chatham Dockyard, continued to grow. By the late 18th century this development on the borders of Gillingham and Chatham had about 400 houses, 'most of which have been erected within the memory of people now living', and was described by the local historian Hasted as 'a spot remarkable as well for the healthiness of its situation, as the beauty of the prospect, a large village or rather from the size and populousness of it, a town'.[5]

Between 1780 and 1820 both Chatham and Rochester expanded to the south, providing prestigious new housing for those who wished to escape from the increasingly overcrowded and dirty town centres. For the middle classes in Chatham there was the opportunity to move into new houses such as those on Ordnance Terrace. This was an option taken up by John Dickens, the father of the novelist Charles Dickens. The Dickens family moved to Chatham when John took up post as a clerk to the Pay Office in the dockyard. Earning a good salary of £200 a year, he rented the house, which had three floors and a cellar, at a cost of £80 a year. Although today Ordnance Terrace overlooks Chatham Railway station, when Dickens lived there it looked out over a wheat field and was backed by the chalk hills. The family's stay in these pleasant surroundings was short-lived. By 1821 they had moved to a far less impressive house in the Brook in the centre of Chatham, clearly signalling a lack of funds.[6]

Another significant development was the prestigious housing built along New Road in Chatham between 1790 and 1820, much of which survives today. The road was begun in 1791 following the Act of Parliament for cleaning and lighting Chatham's streets and completed with the building of a viaduct over Rome Lane (now Railway Street). New Road was designed to bypass Chatham High Street and joined with New Road Rochester to form the main road between London, Canterbury and Dover.

Figure 65 Ordnance Terrace, Chatham. Like many buildings in the Medway Towns of similar date, it was fronted in brick but otherwise built of timber. No. 11 was the home of the Dickens family from 1817-21.

Figure 66   The Brook in the centre of Chatham, which took its name from a stream that by 1800 had become an open sewer. The second house from the left was the Dickens' family home from 1821-2.

The land on which New Road was built was owned by two men, Thomas Whittaker and James Best of the local brewing family. In 1793 Whittaker leased his property at the eastern end of the road to a bricklayer, Thomas Milton, and a house carpenter William Mannering. A requirement of the lease was that houses would be built on the land within three years. Over the next 12 years Milton and Mannering built houses to a variety of designs on both sides of New Road. James Best developed the western end of the road, beginning with the building of Gibraltar Terrace on the south. A central block of four houses was built first – the pediment of the building is dated 1794 – followed by more building to the east and then a western extension in the early years of the 19th century.

The respectable person who wished to escape from the increasingly crowded High Street area of Rochester had, from

Figure 67   Gibraltar Terrace, dated 1794, one of the varied terraces of houses along New Road, Chatham, built in stages between 1790 and 1820.

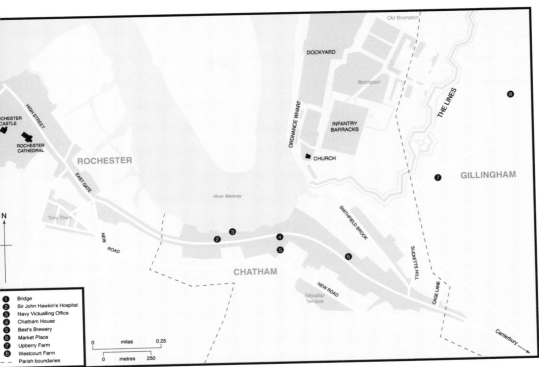

①	Bridge
②	Sir John Hawkin's Hospital
③	Navy Victualling Office
④	Chatham House
⑤	Best's Brewery
⑥	Market Place
⑦	Upberry Farm
⑧	Westcourt Farm
- -	Parish boundaries

Figure 68 Map showing the location of the new suburb of Troy Town as well as areas of new building on New Road, the expansion of Brompton to the south of Old Brompton and key buildings along the old London-Dover road.

the 1780s, the option of seeking accommodation in another new suburb which grew to the south of the city in the parish of St Margaret's. This residential development was initiated by a Chatham wine merchant, John Cazeneuve Troy, who owned the land and let it on building leases in the same way as Best and Whittaker did on New Road. New streets were laid out in a regular grid pattern and the area became known as Troy Town. By the 1830s it was being described as 'a large cluster of neat and substantially built houses'.[7]

The move to create these suburbs for the more affluent inhabitants was prompted by the sharp increase in the population of the Medway Towns in the late 18th and early 19th centuries. The existing housing stock was subdivided, causing overcrowding in the town centres. Those who could afford to move out were eager to occupy more spacious and exclusive newly built homes.

Population

After the depression of the 1720s the population of the Medway Towns had grown steadily, but in the 1790s the pace quickened. Much of this late 18th-century growth can be attributed to the demands of war increasing the dockyard workforce. The number of employees in Chatham Dockyard increased by about 25 per cent in the period

Figure 69 Population
of the Medway Towns,
1801-21.

	1801	1811	1821
Strood	2,334	2,504	2, 704
Rochester	5,645	6,566	7,552
Gillingham	4,135	5,135	6,209
Chatham	10,505	12,652	15,268
Total	22,619	26,857	31,733

1775-95 and those in the victualling yard by 30 per cent. When war
with France broke out in February 1793 an additional 200 workers
were taken on in the yards. During the 18th century the population of
Chatham had more than trebled. Chatham's rapid growth outstripped
that of Rochester, the county and the nation where the population
had doubled in this period. By 1801 one quarter of Kent's population
lived in the ports on the Thames and the Medway.[8]

Census figures for the first 20 years of the 19th century show
that, in common with the rest of Britain, the population of
the Medway area continued to expand rapidly. The combined
population of the four communities increased by nearly 50 per
cent. Rochester, Gillingham and Chatham experienced the most
significant growth. Strood, the smallest in number, saw only a
modest increase, suggesting that it was least affected by the growth
of industry in Chatham Dockyard.

Town Life

Visitors' accounts of their stay in the area provide us with some
insight into the facilities available in a provincial town at the end
of the 18th century. Both John Gale Jones and John Byng, Lord
Torrington, made use of Gilman's library in Rochester. Byng visited
'the fine shop of Mr G' before breakfast on the second day of his
stay in Rochester in 1790, noting that the owner was 'a talking
bustling Fellow ... our Distributor of Stamps for the W. Division
of Kent'. That evening he returned to the library to read the day's
newspapers before bed. Six years later Jones 'visited the circulating
library, which I found very convenient, as the London papers arrive
there every day by three o'clock in the afternoon. Here such of the
inhabitants who choose to subscribe assemble together in a little
back parlour, to converse and to read the news.'[9]

Jones also visited the assembly rooms in Chatham, an essential
feature of polite town life in the late 18th century. He sought
conversation with 'what was usually termed the higher and more
polished classes of civilised society ... excited ... as well by a
fondness for dancing as from a motive of political curiosity'. He
was pleased with what he found: 'every thing bore the aspect of
politeness and good sense', but was also surprised to find that,

'Chatham being a military town', there were no soldiers present. He was told that 'in consequence of a disturbance having taken place', the military were now excluded from the assembly. Navy men were admitted only if they did not wear their uniform and were introduced by a friend who would vouch for their good behaviour.[10]

The military and naval presence

The many-faceted impact of the military and the naval complex on the day-to-day life of the town is also evident. On a couple of occasions Jones described how he heard 'The drum and fife, with merry note, calling the soldiers from their barracks to the morning parade', and that this 'shook the distant air with tremulous vibrations'. William Cobbett, recalling his teenage years, 'his cap and feather days' as a soldier in the Medway area, remembered how the pretty young women of the town had done 'their best to smooth the inequalities of life, and to give us "brave fellows", as often as they could, strong beer, when their churlish masters or fathers or husbands would have drenched us to death with small'.[11] The consequences of this kindness were not viewed so fondly by another contemporary. On recalling a walk up Chatham Hill in 1797, William Hone remembered the *Star* inn with its splendid views over the Medway, and a particular day when sailors and their shipmates spilled from the inn, 'drinking grog out of pewter mugs and earthen basins, and vociferating "Rule Britannia"', but he suggested that on many occasions the consumption of alcohol at the *Star* was excessive and the consequences unpleasant. The inn was 'in war time the constant scene of naval and military orgies, and therefore repelled rather than courted other visitants'. He hastened to add that by 1827 it was 'a respectable inn and a stage for the refreshment of coach travellers'.[12]

The port also brought a cosmopolitan air to the local community, although it seems that foreigners were not always welcomed. Russian sailors, whose ships had been sent to Chatham for repair, were regarded with suspicion by the local people, who believed that this was a ploy to allow the Russians to spy on the yards and the defences. Anti-Russian feelings were also inflamed by 'a circumstance ... which excited a great deal of resentment':

The victualling office had sent a considerable quantity of beef on board the Russian vessels, for the use of the sailors, but either from its not being sufficiently salted, or for some other trifling reason, they threw the whole into the river, whence it was picked up by the inhabitants in boats, and afterwards sold in the town!

Figure 70 The continuous open interior of the ropery in Chatham Dockyard, over 1,100 feet long, showing some of the original equipment. Rope was wound by twisting the strands together on a forming machine mounted on a wheeled carriage (in the distance and right), which ran down the building. Hand power was used until a Boulton & Watt engine was installed c.1836.

This, with some other particulars which he related, such as the children pointing at them in ridicule, whenever they passed in the streets, and calling out to them, Roos, Roos! And their troublesome behaviour in the various shops to which they had occasion to resort, afforded a strong apprehension that some serious disturbance would take place between the inhabitants and themselves before they quitted the town.[13]

Innovation in Chatham Dockyard

Figure 71 The engine house and brick chimney, 140 feet high, of the steam-powered saw mill in Chatham Dockyard. To the left are the 19th-century offices. The mill was part of a sophisticated process which brought timber from the mast pond by canal and delivered it to the timber seasoning sheds.

The Napoleonic Wars created an additional demand for warships. Even before the conflict with France began in 1793, naval authorities recognised that the facilities at Chatham Dockyard needed updating if the yards were to be able to support the navy. Crucial to the fitting of any ship was the rope needed for rigging, with each ship using up to 20 miles of rope. Rope had been made at Chatham Dockyard since 1612 but with ever increasing demand the ropery was extended between 1786 and 1812, creating the building that stands today. The new building measured 1,135 feet and was able to make a rope 720 feet long. New technical innovations were introduced, including a mechanical rope-making machine, designed by Henry Maudslay, in 1811.

Another innovation prompted by the demands of war was the introduction of a block-making machine and a saw mill, both powered by steam and performing work previously been done by hand. Samuel Bentham, Inspector General of Naval Works, saw the potential of steam power and brought in Marc Brunel, a French engineer, to design and build the machines. The block-making machine, which made encased pulleys, essential for the management of ship's rigging, was first introduced at Portsmouth and brought to Chatham Dockyard in 1807. Work then began on building a saw mill to speed up the processing of the 12,000 tons of timber imported to Chatham every year for shipbuilding.[14]

As well as meeting the increased demand for repairs and refits caused by naval conflict, the shipbuilding yards at Chatham constructed 14 new ships in the period 1793-1815, while Britain was at war with France. Although the workforce was increased, there were also periods when workers were ordered to work double shifts and Sundays. As the pressure grew, work was also put out to the smaller private shipyards in the area. Muddles' yard in Gillingham, and Nicholson's and Crump's in Rochester, were where warships such as the *Aimable* were repaired and HMS *Spartan* was built, although these yards were more accustomed to handling merchant shipping.[15]

Defences

The war with France once again raised the issue of security in the Medway, with growing fears that the French army would invade England, landing on the Kent coast. As the Rochfoucauld brothers noted on their tour of England in 1785, Chatham was already surrounded by 'a semi-circular entrenchment, which runs eastward to a stone fort not yet quite finished'. In their view the Lines and Fort Amherst were of limited use in protecting Chatham Dockyard from an armed force attacking from the land. They would 'safeguard the dock and shipyard unless a body of troops arrived in force'. The threat of a French invasion prompted a significant extension of military defences, with the construction of additional barracks to house the steadily increasing military presence in the area.[16]

Figure 72 Engraving of a view over Chatham, Rochester and Strood painted in 1832 by J.M.W. Turner. Turner was looking west from Fort Amherst, with Fort Pitt in the distance to his left.

The south-east of England was the most likely invasion point for the French troops gathered just over the Channel in Calais and, as the Dutch invasion of 1667 had demonstrated, the Medway was vulnerable. In 1803, Prime Minister William Pitt ordered the strengthening of defences in Medway, Dover and Romney Marsh. This resulted in additional building at Fort Amherst and was followed by the construction of Fort Clarence, completed in 1812, and of Fort Pitt, finished in 1819.

Additional defences required additional troops to man the fortifications and they in turn required accommodation. New Marine barracks had been built in the 1770s on Dock Road between the southern end of Chatham Dockyard and St Mary's church. Between 1804 and 1806 Artillery Barracks, known today as Brompton Barracks, were built overlooking the dockyard to house 1,200 men, with separate accommodation for officers. Much of the labour force needed for this new building was drawn from convicts and French prisoners of war held on the prison hulks moored on the river Medway. St Mary's Barracks, built in 1808-12, was originally designed to hold French prisoners of war and only later became a military barracks.

In 1812 the Royal School of Engineers was established in Brompton Barracks with Captain Charles Pasley as its first director. His experience in the Peninsular War had highlighted the need for men to be better trained in constructing and breaching military defences and Brompton offered good opportunities for practising skills such as sapping, mining, earth moving and river crossing.[17]

Figure 73 The upper gallery of the Dockyard church, built in 1808-11 to designs by Edward Holl, architect to the Navy Board. Its interior, with wide well-lit gallery, follows the pattern of Nonconformist chapels, giving all an opportunity to see and hear the preacher.

Figure 74 The medieval parish church of St Nicholas, Strood, was rebuilt 1812-14, incorporating the original west tower. The new work in simple classical style was designed by (Sir) Robert Smirke, later architect of the British Museum.

Figure 75 Zoar chapel at Strood, built for a dissenting congregation in 1786. The brick front had simple gothic details.

Religious practice

As the local population grew, adequate facilities for worship in the Medway communities were needed. Much building and rebuilding of churches and chapels was done during the late 18th and early 19th centuries. St Mary's church in Chatham underwent considerable remodelling during the course of the 18th century. By the 1740s the congregation had outgrown the building, which was in need of repair. Some improvements were carried out, but further modifications were thought necessary in the 1780s when the nave and chancel were demolished and rebuilt. Even then there were fears that the overcrowded congregation would migrate to the nonconformist chapels, prompting the building of a new Anglican church in Chatham Dockyard in 1808-11.[18]

In Strood, the old parish church of St Nicholas was found to be in a serious state of disrepair and was demolished in 1811. The foundation stone for a new church was laid the following year and the building opened for worship in 1814. This exercise caused considerable long-term debt to the parish and, writing at the end of the 19th century, Henry Smetham, a local historian, mourned 'the loss of an ancient and picturesque edifice … in its stead they erected the present unsightly structure which has the dubious merit of being amongst the ugliest churches in the kingdom … Happily the tower, save outward embellishment, was left intact'.[19]

Despite the efforts of the Anglicans to provide new churches, the large influx of soldiers and dockyard workers during the Napoleonic Wars swelled the ranks of nonconformist worshippers in the Medway area. This was not a new religious mood: there is evidence of nonconformity in the Medway area from the 17th century, with established Congregationalist, Baptist and Quaker communities. During the latter half of the 18th century Methodist worship became popular among the dockyard workers and also recruited well from the ever-growing military presence.

John Wesley first preached in Gillingham at Brompton in October 1753, offering two services to 'a serious congregation', one in the evening and one at five the following morning before work started in Chatham Dockyard. He visited again in 1767 and in 1769. A subscription was opened for the building of a chapel, but in Wesley's words there was 'a poor showing': only £3 9s. 2¾d. was collected. Services led by local men continued to be held in the barracks until a Wesleyan chapel was built in Rochester in 1770. A second chapel, more convenient for the dockyard and barracks, was opened in Manor Street, Brompton, in 1788. Its congregation soon outgrew the building, which was enlarged in 1810. The village of Gillingham gained its own Wesleyan chapel in 1795 on Christmas Street.[20]

Religious Life

The Religious Census of 1851 revealed that nearly half the population of England did not attend any place of worship; it also highlighted the extent of nonconformity. Only half of all worshippers attended Church of England services and the Medway Towns were no exception to this. Religious dissent there had grown steadily since the 17th century and by the mid-19th all the towns had well-established Nonconformist churches and chapels. The new places of worship offered an attractive contrast to the medieval parish churches, both in the quality of the accommodation they offered and in the evangelical message they preached to the Medway's industrial workers.

Perhaps not surprisingly, Anglicanism predominated in the cathedral city of Rochester and neighbouring Strood, attracting around 70 per cent of churchgoers. Rochester's parish churches of St Nicholas and St Margaret drew most of them, and the cathedral and St Nicholas at Strood had much smaller congregations. The cathedral was rather exclusive, offering few seats to those not connected to its chapter, while the incumbent of Strood parish church noted that 'I think it right to state that the parish of Strood has been subjected to many years of spiritual neglect'. Dissenters – including the Society of Friends, Independents, Baptists and Wesleyan Methodists – had places of worship in Rochester and Strood, where the Zoar Independent chapel was popular. There was also a small Jewish community in the Medway with a synagogue on Rochester High Street.

In Chatham and Gillingham, support for Dissent was stronger, reflecting the greater concentration of industrial workers, always a fertile ground for nonconformity. In Chatham, despite the provision of four new churches in the first half of the 19th century, less than half of church attendances was at one of the six Anglican churches in the parish. The choice for those wishing to worship outside the Church of England was wide: Independents, Baptists, Unitarians, Bible Christians, and Wesleyan and Primitive Methodists all had a presence. There were also small Roman Catholic, Swedenborgian and Catholic Apostolic congregations.

Gillingham's St Mary Magdalene was small and some way away from the military and dockyard presence in the west of the parish. To cater for the spiritual needs of that rapidly increasing population, in 1848 a new parish of Brompton was formed and Holy Trinity church was built, providing seating for over a thousand. St Michael's Roman Catholic church in Brompton was also well attended, but it was the Wesleyans who had the greatest support in Gillingham, with over half of the attendances recorded in the 1851 census being at one of the three Wesleyan chapels in the parish.

In the second half of the 19th century, the Church of England responded to the challenge of catering for the rapidly increasing population by continuing to create new parishes and building 10 new churches: three each in Rochester, Chatham and Gillingham and one in Strood. Despite those efforts, nonconformity continued to flourish, particularly among the dockyard workers in Gillingham. Migrants from all over England brought with them a wide range of religious beliefs and by the late 19th century there were more than twenty different nonconformist congregations in Gillingham, most unusual being the Jezreelites.

Figure A   *Chatham Memorial Synagogue in the High Street, on the border between Rochester and Chatham. It replaced in 1861 what Bagshaw's Street Directory of Chatham (1847) referred to as being 'a small building of brick and wood, about one hundred years old, with a clock, visible from the High Street, noteworthy for having a face with Hebrew characters'.*

Anglican churches built after 1850

Rochester

St Peter, King Street. Church built 1858-60, demolished 1973; parish created 1860 from Rochester St Nicholas. Original registers from 1860.
Borstal, St Matthew, Borstal Street. Church built 1878; parish created 1901 from Rochester St Margaret. Original registers from 1879.
St Andrew, Cossack Street. Mission church, built 1889. Original registers from 1890.

Chatham

Luton, Christchurch, Luton Rd. Church built 1884, replacing 1843 building; parish created 1842 from Chatham St Mary. Original registers from 1852.
St John the Divine. Church built 1821-2; parish created 1852 from Chatham St Mary, abolished 1964. Original registers from 1853.

St Paul, New Rd. Church built 1853-5, redundant 1974 and demolished; parish created 1855 from Chatham St Mary. Original registers from 1855.

Gillingham

New Brompton, St Mark, Canterbury Street. Church built 1864-6, replacing wood building (1862); parish created 1863 from Gillingham St Mary. Original registers from 1863.
New Brompton, St Barnabas, Nelson Rd. Church built 1889-90, succeeding mission of 1886; parish created 1892 from Gillingham St Mary and New Brompton St Mark. Original registers from 1873.
Lidsing, Chapelry within Gillingham St Mary. Original registers from 1840.

Strood

St Mary, Vicarage Road. Church built 1868-9; parish created 1896 from Strood St Nicholas and Frindsbury. Original registers from 1869.

Sources:
N. Yates, 'Worship in the cathedral, 1540-1870', in N Yates (ed.), *Faith and Fabric: a history of Rochester Cathedral 604-1994* (1996), 145-5; W.N. Yates, 'The major Kentish towns in the Religious census of 1851', *Archaeologica Cantiana*, 100 (1984), 420; M. Roake (ed.), *Religious Worship in Kent: the census of 1851* (Maidstone, 1999), 84-5, 91-105.

Figure B   *Holy Trinity, Military Road (later Maxwell Road), Old Brompton, seen from the corner of Mansion Row and the Sally Port. Erected in 1848 at the expense of the Rev. William and Miss Conway, it was designed in the Early English style by Sir Gilbert Scott Giles. Of brick with stone dressings, it could seat a thousand. It was demolished about 1960.*

Further testimony to the growing popularity of nonconformist worship was the Zoar chapel over the river in Strood, built in 1786 on the south side of the High Street near to Rochester bridge. According to a church history, there was 'great opposition' to the establishment of 'preaching' in Strood, but 'A congregation, however, assembled in a house fitted up for the purpose of public worship, which was named "Strood Tabernacle" … And a Church of Christ was formed on the 5th day of January 1785.' By February of the following year the congregation had begun the work required for the building of a new place of worship. 'It was said such was the zeal of the poor of the congregation, that they freely gave their labour in taking down the old meeting house, removing the materials, and rendering every service in their power, to save expense and forward the work.' Where expertise rather than hard labour was required, the local builder Richard West was paid £142 1s. 5½d. for 'Bricklayers and Plasterers Work & c. To Rebuild the House.'[21]

Popular protest

John Gale Jones' visit to the Medway Towns was not a pleasure trip. He was a political activist whose purpose was to spread the ideas of the London Corresponding Society and to gain support for its demands for universal suffrage and its opposition to press gangs as a means of naval recruitment. The Medway area provided fertile ground for such radical ideas, because of the large number of labourers and artisans employed in Chatham Dockyard and private shipyards and the substantial seafaring population. When Jones arrived in Kent in February 1796 there were already around 200 members of the United Corresponding Society of Rochester, Chatham and Strood.

Figure 76 John Gale Jones. His account of a visit to the Medway area in 1796 offers much detail about life in the local communities.

The London Society and its branches throughout England were also opposed to the so-called Convention Acts. These were part of the government's efforts to control the public discontent which simmered throughout the country in the 1790s because of the cost of the war with France, high inflation and rising food prices, all of which affected the Medway area. The acts were passed in 1795, banning unlicensed public meetings of more than 50 people and changing the law on treasonable acts to include the written and spoken word.[22]

The year before Jones arrived, 1795, was an unsettled time throughout England, and the Medway Towns were no exception. It had been a particularly cold winter; food was in short supply and increasingly expensive. At the end of March there was a food riot in Chatham's Saturday market. The *Kentish Gazette* reported 'that many people of all classes assembled at our market on Saturday last and compelled the butchers to sell their meat at 4d. and others at 4½d. per pound. Some of the soldiers very imprudently joined them.' The following week the Middlesex militia were moved from Medway: 'The order is supposed to be a consequence of some of the men joining the mob at the market.' A couple of days later the East Norfolk militia arrived in Chatham 'to prevent any tumultuous proceedings and the Magistrates have appointed to hold a special sessions tomorrow, being market day'. On market day these troops were also joined by the 11th Light Dragoons from Canterbury and they returned on the two following Saturdays. There were no subsequent disturbances, although this may be explained by the troops' presence; their 'hostile appearance (their swords being drawn) had a very great effect on the public'.[23]

In parallel with the protest about the price of meat, the 600 shipwrights employed in Chatham Dockyard went on strike at the end of March, outraged at the order to use house-carpenters 'to finish the officers' cabins in order to hasten the fitting of the ships which was ever before done by the shipwrights'. Within three days the authorities had dismissed the strikers. The dispute continued for a month, with agreement finally being reached that house-carpenters should only be used in war-time.[24]

Later in the year opposition to the Convention Bills was expressed throughout the area. The newly elected mayor of Rochester, Richard Thompson, drew up a petition opposing the bills and put it in the Guildhall for all to sign. In due course 1,545 signed. Many of the signatories were dockyard workers. On 18 November a handbill appeared on the walls of the dockyard protesting that these new laws, if passed, would:

completely deprive the People of the Liberty of speech, of writing, printing, preaching, or assembly in any respect whatever to obtain redress of Grievances however arbitrary or oppressive without the presence of a Magistrate.

The Commissioner of Chatham Dockyard attempted, but failed, to get the workers to sign a petition asking the King to pass the Convention Bills. Instead they marched *en masse* to the Guildhall and signed the mayor's petition. When the MP for Kent, Filmer Honeywood, came to collect the petition to take it to Parliament, he was met by cheering crowds who pulled his carriage through the streets. On another occasion, according to Jones, crowds gathered to carry an effigy of the bishop of Rochester through the streets in protest at his comment to the House of Lords that 'The people have nothing to do with the laws but to obey them!' Having paraded the effigy around the town, it 'was led into a large field, and committed to the flames, amidst the loud acclamations of the surrounding multitudes'.[25]

Given the purpose of his visit, it is not surprising that Jones was alert to evidence of support for his cause. On the mantelpiece of a 'shrewd, sensible man' he saw 'written in large and legible characters, "National debt £75 a minute, sleeping or waking"'. During a walk from Chatham to Gillingham, his local companions 'expiated on the numerous barracks and fortifications which every where surrounded us, lamented their enormous expences and ridiculed the idea of their being useful either to prevent an invasion from without or quell a general insurrection within'. When attending the Assembly Jones 'learned that the general sentiment of the inhabitants of Rochester, Chatham, and even all of Kent, was decidedly against the present Minister and the present war'.[26]

It should not be inferred from this that the Medway Towns were a hotbed of sedition. The Rochester city minute books give evidence of loyal addresses to the Crown. In June 1792 the corporation expressed its

abhorrence of the many wicked and seditious publications, that have been industriously dispersed throughout the Kingdom, calculated to disturb the peace and happiness of your Majesty's faithful subjects; to weaken their obedience to the wholesome provisions of law and government, and to alienate their minds from a due sense of the blessings they enjoy.

Later the same year the authorities were dismayed to read a report in the papers which suggested that the Patriotic Society at Rochester, England, had sent a message of support to the National Convention in France. Enquiries were made throughout the town but no such society was found to exist. To prevent any further embarrassment, the corporation let it be known that they would be co-operating fully with local magistrates to suppress all seditious meetings and insisted that this intention should be published in the London newspapers.[27]

When Jones arrived in the town he was closely watched by the authorities, who suspected that Jones had been 'sent down to Rochester for the purpose of stirring up sedition'. The claim was made that he would fail: 'inhabitants of Rochester were good loyal subjects and firmly attached to the King and constitution'. Jones was also warned that the manager of the postal service in Rochester had sought permission from the Secretary of State to intercept and read all Jones' mail. It was suspected, but never proved, that Jones played a part in instigating the mutiny at the Nore, just off Sheerness, the following year.[28]

Fire

While war and popular discontent played a significant part in
shaping the experiences of the Medway Towns at the turn of the
19th century, probably the most shocking event for the inhabitants
was the fire that swept through central Chatham on 30 June 1800.
The blaze started on the riverbank to the north of the High Street
in a timber-built shed full of highly combustible materials – ropes,
hemp and oakum, much of which had been tarred. The weather
was hot and dry and had been so throughout May and June, adding
to the danger ever-present in towns which consisted predominantly
of timber-built houses. The fire was discovered about 11 a.m.
Within minutes the flames engulfed the neighbouring warehouse
and forge and a hoy moored at the wharf.

The control and eventual extinguishing of the fire was only
achieved by a concerted communal effort. William Jeffries, a local
lawyer who wrote an account of the day, recalled that:

> The exertions which were made to extinguish the fire can
> scarcely be described. The inhabitants of the town and
> neighbourhood seemed to vie with each other who should
> do most to assist the unhappy and distressed sufferers in the
> removal of their effects, and in the prevention of their houses
> from being consumed, and in so doing exposed themselves to
> severe fatigue and imminent dangers.[29]

One of the problems faced by the firefighters was lack of water.
The fire started within an hour of low tide, preventing the use of
river water. Assistance came from all quarters. Dockyard workers
and the dockyard fire engines were sent along with a supply of
water in butts. Troops helped by putting out the fire and removing
and guarding property from burning homes. Workers, water and
fire engines came from the victualling office and the local brewers
sent water to douse the flames and beer to quench the thirst of
the firefighters.

Within three hours, 97 buildings had been destroyed and
over a hundred families had lost homes and possessions. By
the end of the day, four people had died. Sparks from the fire
'carried a considerable distance, and on reaching the ground, did
considerable injury to the hay, which lay half made, and the hay-
stacks in the fields on the south side of the town'. Also 'two or three
cottages and a barn, at the distance of quarter of a mile at least
from the town, caught fire, and … were in a very short space of
time … consumed.'[30]

In the immediate aftermath of the fire the homeless were
housed in tents provided by the troops and set up in a field next

Figure 77 William Jeffries' plan (south at top) of the properties on Chatham High Street and Heavyside Lane affected by the fire of 1800. Louches Field, to the south of the town, was the site of the cottages and barn which burned down.

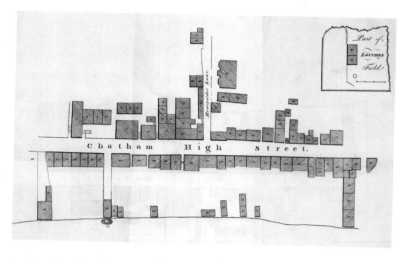

to New Road, and a guard from the local militia, the Chatham and Rochester Volunteers, was set to guard possessions removed from the fire. Within three days a committee was set up by 'several gentlemen of the town' to provide relief for those who had suffered as a result of the fire. Door-to-door collections were organised in Chatham, Rochester and Strood and letters were also sent to communities around the county asking for subscriptions. Over £2,000 was collected and distributed to those who lost possessions and homes in the fire.

Between 1780 and 1820 the Medway Towns, like the rest of Britain, felt the impact of international warfare, bad weather and poor harvests. Chatham housed more and more soldiers, there to safeguard the town and indeed the nation, against the threat of a French invasion. Chatham Dockyard worked under pressure to produce and repair the warships needed to fight France on the high seas. Tensions were evident in the local community in the 1790s as food supplies became scarce and expensive and the Navy Board became nervous as dockyard workers went on strike to improve their working conditions and wages. To make matters worse, fire destroyed homes and livelihoods in 1800 and 1820.

Despite the problems, and in the case of Chatham, perhaps because of the pressures of war, the communities on the banks of the Medway continued to thrive with steady population growth and the building of smart new suburban housing to allow the middle classes to escape the overcrowded centres of Chatham and Rochester. For the Medway Towns war meant work and profit. The end of the war with France in 1815 heralded another period of economic depression which would last until the 1850s.

Chapter 7

Community life in the Medway Towns, 1820-60

'strong feelings of jealousy and rivalry ... '

Life in the communities on the Medway was not particularly rosy in the forty years after the end of the Napoleonic Wars. The 1820s began with another fire in Chatham. This broke out in the early hours of the morning in a bakery on the High Street. Although not as serious as that of 1800, 36 buildings were destroyed including the *Sun Tavern*, the Best family home of Chatham House and part of the Best brewery. In the 1830s and '40s the towns suffered serious outbreaks of cholera and the permanent military and naval presence brought increasing problems with public order. An economic depression hit Chatham Dockyard as the demand for warships fell and many workers were laid off. Levels of employment there only began to recover in the 1850s.[1]

Against this backdrop of social and economic problems there were some bright spots. Although the dockyard economy was uncertain, there was growth in brick making, lime burning and barge building, prompted by London's demand for building materials to house its rapidly expanding population. Transport links were improved by the rebuilding of Rochester bridge and the arrival of railway links to the capital. On the political front, as a result of the Reform Act of 1832, Chatham became a parliamentary borough with the right to elect one MP. Gillingham, Chatham and Rochester achieved administrative unity in dealing with the poor, forming the Medway Union in 1835. This was one of the few issues

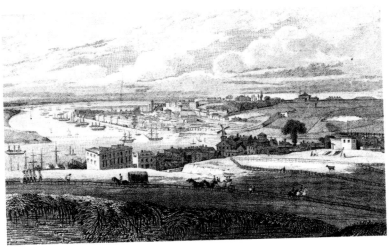

Figure 78 Chatham Dockyard from Fort Pitt Hill in 1828. This view looks out to the north-east over Chatham, the dockyards and Fort Amherst.

upon which the local communities managed to reach agreement. Lawyers sent by the government to collect information for the Commission on Municipal Corporations reported in the same year that the inhabitants of Rochester and Chatham 'entertain strong feelings of jealousy and rivalry and have long done so'.[2]

POPULATION

The number of people who lived in Strood, Rochester, Chatham and Gillingham continued to grow steadily between 1821 and 1861. Between 1800 and 1820 the rate of population growth of the combined Medway Towns had exceeded that of England and Wales, reflecting the economic boost Medway received from the Napoleonic wars. In the 1820s and '30s Medway's growth fell below that of the rest of the country, only to outstrip it again in the 1850s and '60s as Chatham Dockyard began a new phase of expansion. The population of the four communities grew from 31,733 in 1821 to 55,626 in 1861. The period of most rapid growth was the 1850s, when the population grew by around 10,000.

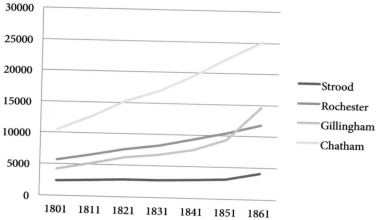

Figure 79   Population of the Medway Towns 1801-61. The beginning of the surge in Gillingham's population in the 1850s is clearly visible, as is the continuing steady growth of Chatham, while Rochester and Strood maintained a lower rate of increase.

Growth rates were somewhat different in each of the four communities. Strood grew slowly compared to its neighbours. Rochester and Gillingham grew at a similar pace until the 1850s, when Gillingham overtook Rochester with a population increase of 50 per cent in the decade. Throughout the period Chatham had the largest population, reflecting the continuing employment opportunities offered by Chatham Dockyard and other related industries. Chatham also had the fastest rate of growth until the 1850s, when it was overtaken by Gillingham as a new wave of dockyard workers came to the area and were housed in New Brompton.

Migration

While some of this growth can be attributed to an improvement in living conditions, Gillingham and Chatham had become magnets for migrants seeking work in Chatham Dockyard. An analysis of the 1861 census for New Brompton, the rapidly growing suburb of Gillingham, shows that people travelled from all over the United Kingdom. One third of the population of this area came from outside the county of Kent. Most of those who came from elsewhere were from the southern coastal counties (nine per cent). Many of those that moved to the Medway area were skilled dockyard workers; shipwrights, carpenters and rope makers came from Portsmouth and Plymouth and from the east coast ports, and there were a number of shipwrights from Pembroke in Wales, home of another government dockyard.

Of the two thirds of the population of New Brompton that were born in Kent, three quarters came from one of the Medway Towns. Most of this group had been born in Gillingham but about one fifth came from Chatham. Very few migrated from Rochester and only one family made it over the river from Strood – William Waller, a 27-year-old butcher, his wife Victoria and their infant son Charles were recent arrivals. The remainder of migrants from the county of Kent were mostly from coastal towns, for example, Woolwich, Sheerness and Gravesend. Otherwise people came in small numbers from all over the county. All were drawn to the Medway by the employment opportunities offered by Chatham Dockyard.

THE GROWING TOWNS

As the four Medway communities expanded to house a growing population, each maintained a distinct identity. Contemporary descriptions continued to stress the social superiority and environmental advantages of Rochester, considered by all to be the jewel in the Medway's crown. The cathedral city, as described in 1848, consisted

> principally of one spacious street, intersected by several smaller streets … the houses are in general respectable and of ancient appearance … The city is paved, lighted with gas, and supplied with water conveyed from an excellent spring near a field called the Vines. The environs are extremely pleasant and contain several handsome villas.

Lewis also noted the presence of Troy Town, with 'several streets of neat modern houses', adding that, 'The air is salubrious, and on

Figure 80 Photograph of Strood, 1857, looking across the river from Rochester in the year that the old Rochester bridge was demolished.

the banks of the Medway are beautiful promenades.' Rochester enjoyed a good range of leisure facilities – a theatre, a circulating library and the Medway Bathing Establishment offering 'every accommodation for bathing on very reasonable terms'.[3]

In contrast the 'village' of Strood was said to consist 'principally of one street, on the road from London to Rochester … The houses are irregularly built, and destitute of uniformity and respectability of appearance.' As for Chatham, the town was judged to be 'extensive' but 'irregularly built'. It was acknowledged that the acts for lighting and paving at the end of the 18th century had brought some improvements, but the streets were still judged to be 'narrow and inconvenient for carriages' and the only buildings singled out for praise were the barracks and the officers' houses in Chatham Dockyard.[4]

It was the parish of Gillingham that underwent the most change in this period, particularly during the 1850s. Those writing in the 1830s described the attractive view from the Medway of the original village in the north of the parish:

Figure 81 A view of Gillingham in the early 19th century looking south-west from the river Medway. The village is in the middle distance on higher ground and the tower of the parish church of St Mary Magdalene can be seen slightly to the left of centre.

The houses are prettily situated on elevated ground, removed
a short distance from the water, and afford an attractive
appearance ... the meadow and marshes on the right are
intersected with small creeks, and backed by wooded and
cultivated uplands.[5]

Others dismissed the parish as 'inconsiderable', although it was
recognised that 'at the western extremity of the parish, is the
populous village of Brompton ... chiefly inhabited by artisans and
others employed in the dockyard'.[6]

By the 1850s attention was focused on the boom in house
building that had begun on the farmland between Gillingham
village and Old Brompton to the north of Watling Street to
accommodate the expanding dockyard workforce. John Woodruff,
vicar of the neighbouring parish of Upchurch, on his way to
Chatham in the spring of 1852, noted that:

In walking through Gillingham I was much struck at the vast
number of houses which have sprung up late on the Gillingham
side of the Chatham Lines. New streets have been laid out and
blocks of houses have been erected since last summer which
now form an almost continuous line of streets. I do not know
what name is given to this mushroom town but I suppose it will
be called New Brompton.[7]

Ten years later, this 'mushroom town' was still attracting comment.
In 1862 James Phippen wrote:

Many of the houses are first class in character and the whole
have been erected in a short period – the great numbers daily
increasing that the construction of Aladdin's Palace in a single
day will appear as no longer fabulous to those who here witness
the rapid and intensive conversion of brick and cornfields
into streets, shops, terraces and villas. I was informed by a
respectable builder that homes are occupied before internal
decorations are finished.[8]

The development was a successful speculation for a local landowner, Michael Lock of Woodlands Manor, who had begun to buy
up land from the early 1840s.[9]

The four communities not only had a different look to them, they
were also home to somewhat different social and economic groups.
Judging by the sums of property tax collected in 1842, Rochester
had the wealthiest inhabitants, and Chatham was very much the
poor relation. Not surprisingly, entries in Bagshaws Directory for

The Medway and Gillingham Bathing Establishments

In the 1830s seaside resorts on the north Kent coast were fashionable for the health-giving properties of sea air and sea bathing. Perhaps inspired by the popularity of these resorts, local entrepreneurs in Rochester and Gillingham attempted to capitalise on the tidal flow of the river by opening two bathing establishments.

The first of these, the Medway Bathing Establishment, situated upstream from Rochester Bridge and in the shadow of the castle, opened its doors for business with a grand party on 27 June 1836. A military band played, dinner was provided for 100 local gentlemen, numerous toasts were offered and comic songs were sung for the entertainment of all.[1]

The opening was preceded by an advertising campaign which extolled the virtues of the facilities, the health-giving properties of salt water and the beauty of the surroundings. The main building of Kentish ragstone, designed by London architect Sidney Smirke, was equipped with a 'splendid saloon … offering extensive views up and down the river Medway unequalled for beauty and variety by any scene in the county of Kent'. Up to 12 people at a time could be accommodated in smaller rooms for warm saltwater baths, steam baths and cold and warm showers. In addition to the land-based facilities visitors were also offered 'A floating vessel of fanciful and novel structure' moored on the river 'containing several baths and a general basin of great extent for the accommodation of the expert swimmer and those desirous of acquiring the art'. Customers were assured that the 'strength and saltness' of the water would 'approximate as nearly as possible to the open sea' and that the 'local charms' of the castle, cathedral and chapterhouse, ' together with the facilities of transport to and from London must render this place one of the most favoured for pleasure.'[2]

A year later, the Brompton and Gillingham Bathing Establishment opened near Gillingham Fort. According to a local directory, 'for some time past' efforts had been made to convert Brompton 'and the neighbouring village of Gillingham into a watering-place'. The floating bath consisted of 'bathing rooms; dripping, dressing and attendants rooms, with a

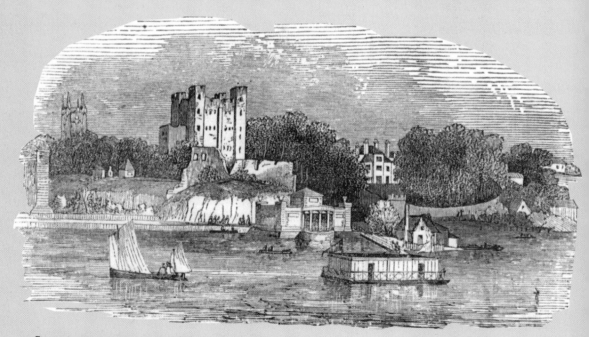

Figure A *The 'floating vessel of fanciful and novel structure' of the Medway Bathing Establishment in its position on the River Medway beneath Rochester Castle*

railed walk all round the machine'. Advertisements for the facility again stressed the health-giving properties of the area, ease of transport to Gravesend and London by road and sea and the local attractions, including ' the continually varying scenes of amusement and interest to be found in the military evolutions of the extensive and well disciplined Garrison of Chatham'.[3]

Unfortunately, neither enterprise flourished. Within six months the Medway establishment was struggling to pay its creditors and the final entry in the company minute books for February 1842 was a plea to shareholders to raise funds to prevent legal proceedings. In 1847 the building was referred to in Bagshaw's directory as a 'medical establishment'. By 1865 the facilities had fallen into disuse, although they enjoyed a revival as public baths from 1880-1935.[4]

According to *Wright's Topography*, the Gillingham venture was more successful. In its first year it offered shareholders a healthy dividend of 10 per cent, and plans were afoot for expansion. What happened next is something of a mystery as no further mention of these baths has been found in the records. The experience of the Medway baths suggests it is unlikely that this attempt at promoting the health-giving properties of the river Medway had any long-term success.[5]

145

THE BROMPTON AND GILLINGHAM

BATHING ESTABLISHMENT,

Consists of an elegant and convenient Floating Machine, with Warm Baths on shore.

THE Water here has been ascertained, by correct analysis, to possess the same properties at High Water as that at the Nore, and to be at all times equally *pure* and *clear*, a circumstance of material importance to all who Bathe, whether it be for the improvement of their health, or in the pursuit of pleasure.

This newly Established Watering Place is situated on the Banks of the Medway, about two miles from Rochester, and nine from Gravesend, from whence coaches, vans, and other carriages, run almost every half hour during the day, while steam-boats, and other vessels, are continually passing and repassing the Bathing Establishment, and it is in contemplation to run vans, or other vehicles, to and from Rochester, Chatham, &c., and the Baths. The Inns and Lodging Houses in the vicinity, afford ample and reasonable accommodations to the visitor and lover of pleasure ; while the beautiful walks and drives amid the enchanting and pleasing scenery of the neighbourhood, the continually varying scenes of amusement and interest to be found in the military evolutions of the extensive and well disciplined Garrison of Chatham, and the great variety of public works too numerous and too important to be mentioned here, combined with the well known salubrity of the air, and the superior efficacy of the water, so admirably adapted to the Valetudinarian, and Delicate Children requiring Sea Bathing, enable the Directors of the above establishment to anticipate, with confidence, an increased share of the public patronage.

The following is the Scale of Charges :—

	s.	d.		£ s.	d.	
Warm Bath	2	0 each or	1	0 0	per doz.
Superior Plunging Bath, for Ladies..	1	0	..	0 10	0	..
Plunging or Swimming Bath....	0	6	..	0 5	0	..
Ditto for Children under ten years of age	0	4	..	0 3	0	..

N.B.—A Waterman will be in constant attendance to convey the company to and from the Bath.—Proper attendance on board for Ladies.

Directions of individuals having apartments to let, may be had at the principal Inns at Brompton and Gillingham, and likewise of any of the Directors, or at the Office of the establishment.

Brompton, 1838.

L

Figure B *An Advertisement for the Gillingham Baths in a local directory for 1838.*

1 *Rochester, Chatham and Strood Gazette* (28 June 1836).
2 *Rochester, Chatham and Strood Gazette* (14 June 1836).
3 *Wright's Topography of Rochester, Chatham, Strood Brompton &c.*, (1838), 117-19,145.
4 MALSC DE279, Rochester Bathing Establishment, 1836-1842.
5 *Wright's Topography*, 118-19

Thanks to Peter Lyons for his detailed research on this topic.

Figure 82 Property tax
collected in the Medway
Towns in 1842.

	Property Tax	Population	Tax per head of population
Rochester	£43,698	8,401	£5.2
Strood	£10,198	2,834	£3.5
Gillingham	£20,330	7,640	£2.6
Chatham	£44,465	18,962	£2.3

1847 suggest that Rochester had the highest proportion of gentry in its population and Chatham the lowest.[10]

Wealth in the towns

Although the wealth profile of the four Medway towns differed, within each there was evidence of the physical separation of various social groups. With the exception of Strood, where the few resident gentry tended to live outside the built-up area, each had developed areas which were almost exclusively the domain of the wealthier, higher-status members of society. The gentry in Rochester tended to cluster around the cathedral precincts and the middle classes lived in Troy Town. In Chatham, Gibraltar Terrace on New Road was firmly established as a high-status residence, as were a few streets in Old Brompton overlooking Chatham Dockyard, which were used by some of the higher-ranking navy and army officers.[11]

Both Strood and Gillingham, on the edges of the urban development, continued to have a significant proportion of people engaged in agriculture. For example, the 1841 census for Strood showed that around one in five of all those whose occupation was recorded was engaged in some kind of agricultural work. Three quarters of this group were agricultural labourers and there were also 20 gardeners, 10 farmers and 13 men employed in milling. This agricultural activity would have played an important part in feeding the townspeople, as would the labour of the 72 fishermen and oyster dredgers.

In contrast, in Old Brompton, which straddled the boundary of the parishes of Gillingham and Chatham, one in eight of the population was of 'independent means' and there was a similar proportion of skilled artisans from Chatham Dockyard, such as shipwrights and ropemakers. The relative wealth of these inhabitants is also evident from the high number of servants in the population and from the presence of those who supplied luxury items. A bookseller and a stationer would have had little trade in a less salubrious area. There was also a significant proportion of military personnel. In 1841 approaching one in 10 of the population of Old Brompton were soldiers living in

private accommodation. The military presence continued to
grow rapidly. By the 1860s more than one third of the population
of the residential streets of Old Brompton were soldiers and
nearly 3,000 military personnel lived in the nearby St Mary's and
Brompton Barracks.[12]

Rochester's largest occupational category was formed by those
engaged in the professions or public service. The cathedral had its
clerics living around it and many dockyard officials preferred to
live in Rochester as did lawyers, teachers and those who held public
office. In 1841 the 'neat modern houses' of Troy Town housed those
of independent means, the collectors of local taxes, naval and army
officers, policemen and the more substantial artisans.[13]

Social Problems

The social mix in the urban environment of the Medway
communities ensured that the genteel did not always feel entirely at
ease when out and about. Henry Coxwell, the son of a naval officer,
who lived in Gillingham, recalled that when as a young man in the
1830s he was asked to chaperone his sisters to a ball in Rochester
'although the highway robbers were not so frequent it was still wise
to be provided with fire arms.'[14]

Peace on the streets was frequently threatened by fighting
between various branches of the militia, or between the militia
and local people. It was not unusual for clashes to end with
fatalities and accounts of such events appear with some regularity
in the local and national press, although it is not always clear who
was at fault. One such altercation took place after the races on
21 August 1834. Two somewhat conflicting accounts appeared
in *The Times*. The first report, picked up from the local press,
spoke of the unbridled violence unleashed on the Chatham Lines
after the race meeting when soldiers from the 88th regiment
launched an unprovoked bayonet attack on the crowds, 'plunging
them indiscriminately into every individual within their reach
thereby wounding about 30 persons … The scene on the lines was
terrific; men women and children were trampled and cut about
in a most horrid manner'. The next day the soldiers launched
another unprovoked attack on sailors outside their barracks, with
five ending up in hospital. The report made it clear that this was
not an isolated incident. 'About three weeks ago this town was
so disturbed by the same regiment that the shopkeepers were
compelled to close their windows.' In response to the violence
the townspeople called a public meeting, protesting strongly at
the soldiers being allowed to carry arms on the streets, and a
petition was presented to the High Constable calling for better

control. A week later another piece appeared in *The Times*, this time originating from the *Naval & Military Gazette*. This claimed that the 'riot' was provoked by the sailors and civilians and that it was the soldiers of the 88th who had been 'ill treated, insulted and forced to act in self defence'. Whoever was to blame, the incident illustrates the tensions that existed on the streets of the Medway Towns.[15]

The towns also offered plenty of opportunities for illegal activity. The port had long provided a convenient escape route for those wishing to hide themselves from the law in London and again the arrival of sailors being paid off from their ships after long voyages provided easy targets for those who wanted to part them from their money. The authorities were prepared to offer substantial rewards to those who helped catch tricksters and fraudsters. For example, a notice of 1835 promised payment of two shillings 'for conviction of rogues and vagabonds frequenting turnpike roads enticing the unwary into playing with thimbles and other instruments at false and illegal games'.[16]

Another problem that would continue to haunt the streets of 19th-century Medway was prostitution. The presence of a permanent military base and the regular arrival of sailors in the town with several months' pay in their pockets provided an ideal market for prostitutes. The justices of the peace were increasingly aware of this issue and from the late 1820s began to post notices warning women and those who assisted them that those who practised or supported this trade would be prosecuted.

> There has of late taken place a great increase of open vice and immorality in the Town of Chatham and village of Brompton through the great number of women of ill fame and their associates … ordered … that upon complaint being exhibited and due proof made before the said justices against any loose and disorderly women of any immorality lewdness or indecency committed by them such women will be punished as the law directs.[17]

Disease

Some areas of the Medway Towns, particularly in the centre of Chatham, were dangerously unhealthy places to live. This was a problem in many of the inner-city areas of England in the early 19th century, but infant mortality rates in the dockyard town were among the highest in the country, with only one in seven children surviving the first year of life. For adults, life expectancy in the town was six years lower than in the surrounding countryside. The problem was largely one of hygiene. In Chatham open sewers ran through the streets in the centre of the town and these fed into the river, which was the main source of drinking water. The streets themselves were filthy. Although the wealthy areas were swept regularly, in poorer streets human and animal faeces and other rubbish accumulated. Smallpox and typhoid were endemic and there were two serious outbreaks of cholera in the area.

Cholera was spread by eating food or drinking water that had been contaminated with bacteria. England suffered three major cholera epidemics in the 19th century – in the 1830s, 1840s and 1860s. The disease was first reported in Kent in the spring of 1832 when a female vagrant from London died in Rochester, followed by the death of a sailor who worked the Chatham to London boats. It then took hold on the prison hulks on the Medway and 80 prisoners died. Despite quarantining the hulk and the good intentions of the instructions circulated by the authorities several years earlier with the advice on how to avoid and treat the disease, cholera spread rapidly throughout the county. With no real understanding that the disease was water-borne, attempts at containing it were unsuccessful. In the Medway area it spread quickly to the dockyard workers, the military and to those living in the unhealthiest parts of town. Over 300 people died from the disease in Chatham alone. It was only with the arrival of cold weather, which killed off the cholera bacteria, that the epidemic eased.[18]

In 1848 a second cholera outbreak took hold and lingered for more than a year. The speed at which the disease could spread and kill is evident from one of the regular reports in the *Rochester & Chatham Gazette*:

> Deaths from cholera at Strood – On 31st Ult at Strood Hill, Henry Wyatt having survived his wife but a few days, she also died of the same disease. Sept 1 Rachael Rowland, residing in the Fair-Field, aged 27 after 14 hours illness. Sept 2 James Relph near Strood Hill, aged 51 after 12 hours illness – same day the wife of Mr Tippett. Sep 3rd Matthew Boorman residing next door to Relph, aged 55 after an illness of 14 hours.[19]

Living conditions improved rapidly in the 1850s with the setting up of a permanent Board of Health. The board investigated and reported on Chatham in 1852, identifying the threats to health of open sewers, dirty streets and contaminated water. Measures to tackle these problems were soon introduced: open sewers were replaced by closed drains, streets were cleaned more effectively and a new water supply was established, taking water from a spring outside the town.[20]

THE LOCAL ECONOMY

Shipbuilding

With the end of the Napoleonic wars, around one third of the workers in Chatham Dockyard were laid off. With the slump in demand for large warships, the yards turned their hand to building smaller vessels – sloops, brigs or fifth rates. These ships were well suited to the changing role of the navy. No longer engaged in warfare at sea, smaller vessels were ideal for patrolling coastlines in the colonies or at home in the fight against piracy and smuggling.[21]

A new method of propulsion was introduced: steam was used first in tugs and then, in the 1830s and '40s, was tested in warships. The advantage of steam was that ships were no longer dependent on wind strength and direction and it also offered particular advantages in terms of speed. Trials of the frigate *Penelope* on the Medway were reported in the local paper. Using only three of her four boilers, 'she gained upon some of the most rapid of the river boats … she proved herself a vessel of extraordinary velocity'.[22]

Other Industries

The decline in the naval shipbuilding sector of the local economy was, to some extent, compensated for by growth in other industries. The Medway Towns need to be considered as part of the general industrial development of the lower Medway valley in the early 19th century, where brick making and lime burning flourished. Providing transport for these heavy building materials also gave a boost to barge building on the riverbanks.

Brickmaking

Clay and chalk, the raw materials for brick making, were readily available in the Medway area. The industry had grown in the area since the 17th century when brick began to replace timber for house building. In the towns much of the brick required for the expansion of housing in the early 19th century would have been made on site. William Ireland noted that 'Troy Town, standing at the back of Rochester, which has sprung up in the last thirty years, occupies a space of ground formerly used as brickfields'. Bricks were also made for export. As London's population expanded in the early 19th century, Medway bricks were sent by barge to meet the demand for house-building and the construction of industrial buildings in the capital.[23]

Figure 83 A brick-making team in Gillingham, c.1905.

The 1841 census records 15 brick workers in Strood and this figure had increased to 109 by 1861. This expansion was the result of Henry Everist, a major manufacturer in the area, bringing most of his production to the Temple Manor site in Strood in the 1840s. Brick makers were rather thinner on the ground in Gillingham. The same census records just one brick maker, employing a man and a boy, in New Brompton.

It was not unusual for whole families to work in brick production and live on or close to the brick fields. For example, in Strood in 1861 Henry Allum (57), his son Thomas (17) and daughters Mary Ann (15) and Elizabeth (12) were all listed as 'labourer in the brickfield' and lived in one of the Ernest Cottages 'in the brickfield'. Only Henry's wife, Mary, and their two youngest sons, aged nine and seven, were not employed in the brickfields.

Barge building

Figure 84 Barges on the Medway, c.1900. The building of barges was a traditional industry on the banks of the lower Medway, the vessels playing an important part in the transport of agricultural produce, bricks and lime from the area to London.

Another industry that Strood shared with other communities in the lower Medway Valley was barge building. Barges had traditionally been used for conveying Kentish agricultural produce to London via the Medway. They were also ideal for transporting heavy goods such as bricks and lime to the capital and beyond and the demand for these vessels grew, along with the industries, in the first half of the 19th century. There is evidence of barge building in several locations on the lower Medway, but most of the barge building in the Medway Towns took place in and around the wharves of Rochester and Strood. The hull of a barge was handcrafted, usually on the bank of the

river, and then additional fittings such as masts, rigging and sails were bought in.[24]

Fishing

Alongside the newer expanding industries, fishing continued to provide a source of income for many families and the boats used by fishermen and oyster dredgers, the bawleys and dobles, were built on the banks of the Medway. Most fishermen continued to be located in Strood. In the 1831 census it was noted that 55 men in Strood and 37 in Gillingham relied on fishing for a living. The 1841 census recorded 72 men engaged in fishing and dredging in Strood. By 1861 this number had declined to 30, reflecting the problems that were to beset that trade in the latter half of the century. Nevertheless, within the jurisdiction of the Rochester Oyster Fishery, which stretched from upriver at Hawkswood out into the estuary as far as Sheerness, a local report stated that there were still 400 men employed as oyster dredgers in the 1860s.[25]

Brewing

The expansion of brick making and lime burning and the continuing employment of dockyard labour combined with the military presence guaranteed a good local market for beer, which was reflected in the number of breweries operating in the towns in the first half of the 19th century. From a listing of six in local directories in 1803, numbers rose to 13 by 1840, falling back to 11 by 1852. These numbers do not include the activities of many small publican brewers who would also have been in operation during this period. Among the larger brewing concerns, Bests continued to lead the pack until the company was transferred to Edward Winch of the *Sun Hotel* in Chatham in 1851.[26]

Transport

The Medway Towns had always profited from proximity to London and good communications with the capital by road and sea. Road links had improved considerably in the final decades of the 18th century as more roads were turnpiked. By 1836 from Rochester and Chatham there were 16 coaches a day travelling to and from the capital. Waterborne traffic took longer to make the journey to London – travelling along the Medway, around the Nore and up the Thames estuary could take up to 24 hours, with adverse wind and weather extending this journey time. This was not a problem for the fleets of barges which carried bricks and other non-perishable items to the capital but was inconvenient

Figure 85 Paddle steamer at Strood Pier, 1859, to the north of Rochester Bridge. From the mid-19th century a service to London operated daily from Strood. The engraving also shows the variety of shipping on the Medway, with barges and fishing boats sharing the river with the paddle steamer.

for human traffic. Journey times by water were improved by the introduction of paddle steamers which went to the capital daily.[27]

In 1824 an attempt was made to improve water communication by cutting a canal through a tunnel from Strood to Gravesend. Hailed by contemporaries as 'one of those triumphs of modern ingenuity', it failed to live up to expectations. The canal was difficult to navigate and the project was not a financial success.[28] The excavation work was not wasted, however. The tunnel was sold to the South Eastern Railway Company who ran a line through it from Gravesend to Strood in 1845. This line took passengers to and from a steamer service from Gravesend to London. Although this proved popular, in 1849 the rail service was extended to Dartford, creating a direct link from Strood to London. In 1858 the railway finally crossed the river Medway and was extended to provide services to Rochester, Chatham and Gillingham and beyond to Canterbury and Dover.

Rochester Bridge

By the 1820s, the state of Rochester's medieval bridge was a matter of some concern. This important river crossing had been repaired and widened between 1792 and 1825 but, though this had brought some improvements for road traffic, it did not solve the problems of shoaling and silting around the foot of the bridge and was a hazard for river traffic, a considerable expense for the Admiralty who paid for the dredging of the Medway. By the 1820s the cost of dredging had risen to around £1,910 a year.

The need for a new bridge was the cause of much political wrangling. Residents feared that they would have to meet the building costs for this venture. Despite some opposition, in 1828 the Bridgewardens resolved that the bridge should be rebuilt and an architect was appointed. Local debates were lengthy and the

Figure 86 Rochester Bridge in 1828, four years after modernisation of the medieval bridge had been completed. The roadway was widened by 12 feet and a footpath was made each side. The width of the cutwaters was reduced so that larger crafts could pass through the arches, and the drawbridge and one pier and arch were replaced with a large central arch.

situation was made more complex by the intervention of two railway companies, the North Kent and the South Eastern, both of whom wanted to build new lines crossing the river at Rochester. Combining the road and rail functions was proposed as a sensible way of reducing costs to all concerned but no agreement was reached. In the end, a design was agreed for a cast-iron structure with an integral swing bridge to allow for the passage of vessels with masts. The Admiralty approved the plan although they retained the right to inspect the progress of the works. Work finally began in 1850 and the new bridge was officially opened on 13 August 1856 with a procession and a firework display.[29]

Perhaps even more spectacular was the demolition of the old bridge, which the Royal Engineers were brought in to mine, blast and dismantle. The *Illustrated Times* ran a feature on the action in January 1854, reporting that the effect of the explosives 'was very striking, the ground for some distance reverberating as if from the effects of an earthquake, while the pier crumbled in pieces and disappeared.'[30]

Figure 87 The old and new bridges between Rochester and Strood, looking towards Strood and depicted in the brief period in which they co-existed. The old bridge was superseded by a cast-iron one with three arches and a ship's passage with a swing bridge. The new bridge, designed by Sir William Cubitt, was begun in 1846 and the old one blown up by the Royal Engineers six months after the new bridge had been completed in 1856.

Figure 88 The first
railway bridge across
the Medway, opened
in 1858 to carry the
Chatham main line of
the London, Chatham
& Dover Railway. It
became disused when
the company merged
to become the South
Eastern & Chatham
Railway and a new, much
grander, bridge was built
in 1892.

POLITICAL CHANGE

Parliamentary representation

The age-old friction between the respective administrations of
Chatham and Rochester came to a head again in the 1830s with
the local discussion and national implementation of the Reform
Act of 1832. Although Chatham's population was twice the
size of Rochester's, they still did not have any discrete political
representation in Parliament. The Reform Act sought to remedy
this situation for the new towns that had emerged in the industrial
revolution of the late 18th and early 19th centuries. The greatest
fear for Rochester was that the inhabitants of Chatham and Strood
would be entitled to vote in the city's parliamentary elections. The
minutes of the corporation's debate on the matter record their view
that this 'would in a very great and most injurious degree affect the
privilege of this city through the preponderating influence which
these places would possess by their larger population'. In short the
electorate of Rochester feared that they would be outnumbered
and overwhelmed by their less civilised neighbours. In the event
they were spared this as Chatham was granted the right to select its
own MP. The first election for the new parliamentary constituency
took place in December 1832, when the Whig candidate, William
Mabberley, was elected.[31]

Local Administration

The next stage in political reform was the report of the Royal
Commission appointed to look at the formation of municipal
corporations throughout England. Representatives of the
Commission visited Rochester and Chatham in 1833. Their visit
was not welcomed by the Rochester Corporation, who resolved

that in his dealings with the commission the Town Clerk should 'give the legal minimum of information'. A local paper reported that 'The alderman and assistants were proved to be a self constituted body uncontrolled by their natural masters, the citizens at large … political bias guided them in almost all their proceedings'.[32]

The Commission's report, published in 1835, indicated that consideration had been given to joining Rochester and Chatham in one municipal corporation but concluded that

> such a step would create a violent dis-satisfaction in both Rochester and Chatham. The inhabitants of the two towns entertain strong feelings of jealousy and rivalry and have long done so; and those feelings were the cause of the absurd system of local acts …[33]

In the circumstances it was agreed that unity was not the way forward.

In 1837 the idea of joining Rochester and Chatham under a single administration was revisited by the Royal Commission on Municipal Boundaries, noting that in their opinion, as the division between Rochester and Chatham was 'a mere arbitrary line', the two communities should be joined under a single jurisdiction. The barrier to this commonsense solution was that 'it would be an unpopular measure with the inhabitants of both towns'. As a result the two remained separate.

The same year saw the first attempt by some of the inhabitants of Chatham to modernise local administration by seeking to replace the existing local authority, the court leet, with a corporation of their own. A committee was formed to look at the pros and cons of attaining borough status and discussions were held with representatives from Gillingham's court leet, but in the end the idea was shelved, probably on the grounds of expense. The estimated annual cost was £330, to be raised from the local ratepayers.[34]

Medway Poor Law Union

Although attempts at imposing overall political unity were not successful, the Medway communities were required to co-operate by the Poor Law Act of 1835. The act brought together all the parishes in Rochester, Chatham and Gillingham under a single poor law administration, forming the Medway Union. Strood, separated by the river from its neighbours, became part of the Aylesford Union. Although later in the century the poor of Medway would be housed in a single workhouse constructed for the purpose in Chatham, initially the existing workhouse buildings were used, separating the various categories of the

poor. Pauper children from the Medway Union were sent to
St Nicholas' workhouse in Rochester and able-bodied men to
St Margaret's, also in Rochester. Women were sent to Chatham
workhouse. The Gillingham workhouse was sold, being thought
too small to be of any use.[35]

LOCAL SPECTACLE

Races on the Chatham Lines

Not all was gloom and doom in the first half of the 19th century. In
addition to the traditional fairs, a grand annual event was the race
meeting held on the Lines in August. Racing took place on the flat
open land outside the fortifications. Robert Pocock recalled that
when he attended in 1822, 'It was windy … there were races for a
plate of £50 when, it is said, twenty thousand persons assembled
and where a poor woman was killed by a horse and cart going over
her.' Sixteen years later *Wright's Topography* reported that this was
still 'a scene of great animation being numerously attended by a gay
assemblage of rank and fashion, there is almost a total suspension
of business for great and small are equally attracted to the stand
and all alike intent on the exciting nature of the sport'.[36]

The entertainment on offer at the races did not meet with the
approval of all. In 1851 an anonymous local resident wrote to
the High Constable expressing concern about the effect on the
female population of the 'disgraceful exhibition of the boxing
men displaying their prowess and in seeing two men knock each
other about'.[37]

Military exercises

Although the presence of the military brought social problems
to the local community, the Royal Engineers also provided
entertainment in the form of military exercises which attracted
large crowds. According to an admiring contemporary:

> The races held on the heights always attracted a gay concourse
> of visitors but the military reviews of more recent occurrence
> are a never failing source of interest and attraction to the
> spectators who muster in their thousands upon these occasions.
> The lively music of the military bands, the bright gaiety of the
> accoutrements and wondrous precision of the evolutions form
> a continuation more calculated than perhaps any other sight in
> England to dazzle the eye and infect the dullest peasant with a
> passion for military glory.[38]

Figure 89 Siege operations on the Lines. Military displays of this kind were a big tourist attraction in the mid-19th century, drawing crowds from the county and the capital, eager to watch the spectacle and excitement of military manoeuvres. In this engraving from the *Illustrated London News* of 1868, spectators are crowded onto the ramparts to the left, overlooking the military operations.

Such spectacles were reported in great detail and with patriotic fervour in the national newspapers. In the summer of 1849 it was estimated that 60-70,000 people had arrived by road, rail and sea to watch the event, streaming in from the Medway Towns, the surrounding countryside and 'extraordinary numbers' from London. The previous year the approach roads to the Lines were completely blocked by spectators.[39]

The changes in the mid-19th-century Medway Towns foreshadowed the events of the following fifty years. The population growth that had begun modestly would escalate to meet the demands of a further expansion of Chatham Dockyard and the other industries that would flourish on the riverbanks. New Brompton, the 'mushroom' community which had put down roots in the 1850s, would become firmly established as home to the dockyard workforce.

Although the local government issues raised in the 1830s had not been resolved by the 1860s, by the end of the century the 'strong feelings of jealousy and rivalry' that had simmered for over two hundred years would be modified. Chatham and Gillingham would take advantage of the opportunities offered by national initiatives to modernise local administration and to stand as equals alongside Rochester.

Chapter 8

Four Towns, 1860-1914

The townscape we see today in the Medway Towns is very much the product of the fifty years leading up to the First World War. In a volume of this size it is not possible to do full justice to the transformation that took place during this period. Although very selective in what is covered, this chapter aims to communicate a flavour of the economic, political and social changes that took place and the impact these had on the local environment.

Much of the change was driven by a series of new demands made on Chatham Dockyard to meet the needs of the British navy in its role in international politics. This prompted a further extension of the yards which required the reclamation of a large swathe of marshland at the northernmost tip of the parish of Gillingham. At the same time the banks of the river Medway in Strood and Rochester became centres of industry for cement manufacture and engineering, much of their output going to support the building boom in late 19th-century London as well as meeting local demand as the built environment of all four towns expanded rapidly. New communities were formed, providing homes for the increased labour force needed to support this rapidly

Figure 90 A view of Rochester Bridge in 1905, painted by marine artist William L. Wyllie. The air pollution from local industry is clearly visible as is the extent of river traffic.

changing industrial scene. The political landscape was altered too, as first Chatham and then Gillingham achieved borough status. From the early 20th century Rochester no longer had the political advantage in the Medway Towns.

A CHANGING ENVIRONMENT

The growth of the cement industry on the banks of the lower Medway had an impact on all who lived in and visited the towns. Other industrial activity clustered on the banks, polluting the river water and filling the air with smoke. A traveller approaching the towns in 1893 described the contrast between the ancient buildings and modern industry:

> As we approach Strood, the fume and incense of kilns, and breweries, and factories come upon us, and it is a busy world we see as we top the hill and look down on the wide Medway, the mingled smoke and steam throwing a haze over the wonderful scene presented by the old Norman Keep that still seems to guard the bridge, and the Cathedral all weathered and brown, and the tangle round about of quaint roofs and dwellings, of closes, courts and fair old gardens.[1]

Some of the smoke and steam came from the railways but most was from the cement works. They were said to cover the area with 'an impalpable white powder'. Arriving in Rochester by train, another commentator noted that the river was 'a silvery sheet of water dotted with brown sails, and bordered by chimneys of the cement and brick industries'. On the riverbank at Rochester:

> all around is boisterous merriment. The noise is deafening. Along the shore are barge-builders, slipways and engineers; and there is a forest of chimneys on the north bank. We catch glimpses of grinding wheels and furnaces. Grey men are loading barges with grey bags. The throb of machinery is everywhere.[2]

Yet, despite the veil of cement dust and the noisy industry on the riverbanks, Rochester maintained its superior gentility, and the beauty of its ruined castle and ancient cathedral compensated for the inconvenience of modern industry in the eyes of most observers. Rochester's continuing social and cultural superiority was evident in the entries in a local directory for 1878. The ancient borough boasted many clubs and societies for the enjoyment and edification of its inhabitants and for the better-off from the surrounding area, eager to take part in urban life. By the 1860s the

A Young Woman's Life in the Medway Towns in 1860

Honoria Roebuck lived with her aunt who ran a small school on Garden Street in Old Brompton. Honoria, aged 16 in 1860, recorded her daily activities and anxieties in a diary throughout this year, offering us a glimpse of life in the Medway Towns in the mid-19th century.

Honoria's life was full, varied and firmly rooted in the local community. As well as helping her aunt with the household chores, in the morning she worked as a private governess for several young boys, the sons of army officers based in the area. In the afternoons she gave music and French lessons to her aunt's pupils and to other young women in Brompton. For the most part she coped with her duties well but on occasion her pupils did not live up to her expectations. '19 June: Gave Miss D a French lesson – too hasty and impatient with her, I fear – she was provokingly stupid – must try not to be so easily irritated.'

Outside her working life Honoria engaged fully in church activities, attending chapel, bible class and helping with charitable activities and bazaars. Her diary entries suggest that she was one of the many nonconformist worshippers in the area, probably a Methodist.

Honoria took advantage of all the facilities offered by the Medway Towns. She enjoyed shopping trips into Chatham and Rochester to buy clothes and ribbons and also went out and about in the local countryside, often walking the hills that circled the area, including an excursion to Strood Hill and back. Leisure pursuits were not confined to the immediate vicinity. Honoria and her aunt made full use of the expanding rail network to move around the county, taking trips to Canterbury and Dover. Honoria also travelled alone by train to stay with friends in London, journeying with confidence and pleasure.

There is no mention of Chatham Dockyard in the diary, although from the end of Garden Street Honoria would have had a clear view over the yards and many of her immediate neighbours were employed there. It seems that the early stages of one of the most significant expansions of the dockyard were of no interest to a middle-class teenage girl.

Figure A   *Pages from Honoria's diary for 1860.*

Figure B   *Honoria's diaries for 1860 and 1862. The latter is written entirely in code and has yet to be transcribed.*

However, military matters were often noted. Her entry for Thursday 1 March 1860 reads, 'Rose at 7. Had grammar and dictation this morning – the Duke of Cambridge came down to lay the foundations of a triumphal arch which is to be erected in Brompton barracks to the memory of the Crimean Heroes.'

Source:
MALSC DE 4096, Diaries of Honoria Roebuck 1860-62. Thanks are due to Astrid Salmon who spent many hours transcribing the diary for 1860.

Figure 91   The chimneys of Strood Cement works on the banks of the Medway show the impact of this industry on the local environment in the early 20th century. There were more than 25 cement works in the Lower Medway Valley at this time.

Rochester Book Society, established in 1797, had two additional off-shoots: the Theological and the Medical Book Societies. More recent additions to the local cultural scene were the Rochester District Philharmonic Union, established 1864, the Horticultural Society, established 1866, and the Rochester and Strood Bible Society. The town also provided a home for the Rochester district branch of the Kent Archaeological Society and for the local Society for the Prevention of Cruelty to Animals, which served the surrounding area. In addition, many worthy clubs and societies were run by the various churches in Rochester.[3]

In contrast, Chatham in 1876 was described as 'a very different style of place to Rochester … a dirty and unpleasant town devoted to the interests of soldiers, sailors and mariners'. The town was said to contain 'little of general interest unconnected with its dockyard or barracks'. It was 'a long dirty street, parallel with the Medway, swarming with soldiers and Jews, and powerfully odorous of shrimps and tobacco'. Chatham, unlike its culturally superior neighbour, was only able to boast offering a home to the Mechanics' Institute, described by Dickens, who gave several lectures there, as 'a most flourishing Institution, and of the highest benefit to the town: two triumphs which I was glad to understand were not at all impaired by the seeming drawbacks that no mechanics belonged to it, and that it was steeped in debt to the chimney-pots'.[4]

INDUSTRIAL CHANGE

Chatham Dockyard extension

In 1854 the French and British joined forces with the Turks in their conflict with Russia in what came to be known as the Crimean war. During this war sea battles had made it clear to the Admiralty that iron-clad battleships were essential to the future success of the

British navy and that the dockyard at Chatham was ideally placed to meet this new challenge. The necessary land for expansion had already been purchased in the 1840s and '50s and work began in 1855 to build a sea wall around the hitherto undeveloped St Mary's Island to the north of the existing complex (Figure 4). In the 1860s the marshland on the island was drained, the ground level was raised by eight feet and foundations were dug for the planned building. This new extension quadrupled the area of Chatham Dockyard from 97 to 380 acres. St Mary's Creek, the narrow waterway that separated the island from the mainland, was turned into three large basins, and four new dry docks were built. Most of the bricks for this extensive construction work were made and fired on site. The transport of materials and goods in and out of the dockyard was made easier by the building of a new railway line in 1877. This branched off from the main London to Dover line, just east of Gillingham station.

Convict labour

Most of the brick making and construction was done by convict labour. Prisoners were housed in a newly built prison on the site of what is now part of the University of Greenwich at Medway. The prison was demolished after the dockyard extension was completed and the prisoners were moved elsewhere. New naval barracks, used today by the university, were built on the site between 1897 and 1903. Up to a thousand prisoners were employed on the dockyard extension at any one time. It considerably reduced the government's labour costs for this extensive and expensive project. When the work was completed in 1885 it had cost around three million pounds.[6]

Figure 92   Construction of the dockyard extension on St Mary's Island as shown in the *London Illustrated News* of 19 September 1868. Much of this was built using convict labour. The expansion quadrupled the size of Chatham Dockyard and provided facilities for the building of iron-clad battleships.

Building iron ships

Initially it was a challenge to find a suitably skilled workforce for
the building of the new iron-clad ships. The problem was that
shipwrights – the skilled artisans who built the ships – were wood-
workers with no experience of metal work. At first the Admiralty
employed iron smiths and boilermakers but after a series of
industrial disputes they were dismissed. Instead the shipwrights
were retrained to work with the new materials.

The size of workforce needed to meet the demands of increased
construction at Chatham Dockyard rose dramatically, although
employment was not always secure. From 1,735 men in 1860 when
the extension began it had risen to 4,199 by the time building work
was completed in 1885. There was a slump in employment in the
late 1880s following a reorganisation of the labour force: over 1,000
men were laid off. The situation improved again from 1889 when
the Naval Defence Act prompted the beginning of the naval arms
race which escalated into the First World War. By 1903 the yard was
employing somewhere in the region of 10,000 workers, a rise which
was directly reflected in the increase in population between 1881
and 1901.[6]

The first two iron-clad ships off the slips were *Royal Oak* in
September 1862 and *Achilles* in December of the same year. The
local paper reported of the launch of *Royal Oak* that 'great interest
has been excited by the event … An immense staging was erected
in the head of the slip; it was decorated with flags.' At 1.30 p.m.
work in the dockyard was brought to a halt and what was 'already
a large crowd was greatly increased by the flocking to the spot of
hundreds of workmen.'[7]

Perhaps even more impressive was HMS *Achilles*, which was
the largest ship in the world at the time. Dickens described the
construction work that he witnessed in the yards;

> Ding, Clash, Dong, BANG, Boom, Rattle, Clash, BANG,
> Clink, BANG, Dong, BANG, Clatter, BANG BANG BANG!
> What on earth is this! This is, or soon will be, the Achilles,
> iron armour-plated ship. Twelve hundred men are working
> at her now; twelve hundred men working on stages over her
> sides, over her bows, over her stern, under her keel, between
> her decks, down in her hold, within her and without, crawling
> and creeping into the finest curves of her lines wherever it
> is possible for men to twist. Twelve hundred hammerers,
> measurers, caulkers, armourers, forgers, smiths, shipwrights;
> twelve hundred dingers, clashers, dongers, rattlers, clinkers,
> bangers bangers bangers![8]

With the extension of the dockyard Chatham once again became, albeit briefly, a major centre for both refitting existing ships and for building new vessels. Many battleships were built of an ever increasing size. In 1875 the *Alexandra* was launched with a tonnage of around 9,000.; in 1905 the *Africa*, with a tonnage of 16,350, was the final battleship to be launched at Chatham. The next innovation in battleships, the Dreadnoughts, were too large for Chatham Dockyard to handle. Subsequently only smaller classes of warships were built there

Submarines

Major job losses in the early 1900s were prevented by yet another innovation in seafaring, the submarine. HMS *C17*, a small submarine powered by a petrol engine, was built in secret at Chatham and launched there in 1908. According to the *Chatham News* the Admiralty had decided to use one of the Royal Dockyards for submarine construction on the grounds of economy, being less expensive than contracting out to private yards, and 'Chatham has been selected because all other new constructions had ceased, except that of a few barges and small craft.'[9] From 1911 to 1914, Chatham Dockyard was kept fully occupied building eight submarines and four cruisers for the navy and also refitting the existing fleet in preparation for war.[10]

Improving the defences

As plans were being laid for the dockyard extension at Chatham in the 1850s, concern was growing about the defence of the realm against attack from the French. A Royal Commission was set up in 1859 which recommended that fortification around the dockyards and anchorages on the Thames and Medway, as well as at Dover, Portsmouth, Plymouth, Portland and Milford Haven, should be upgraded. The report stated that the importance of Chatham Dockyard would be 'much increased when the extensive enlargements to the site ... shall be completed'. It also pointed out that Chatham occupied 'a site of considerable value in a military point of view', being situated on the main road from Dover to London and close to a strategic river crossing at Rochester. The Commission concluded that 'there are abundant reasons for adding very considerably to the existing fortifications'. Improvements to the river defences went ahead but, due to financial constraints, it was not until the 1870s that work started on land. The plan was to build a ring of fortifications around Rochester, Chatham and Gillingham. Work began first on four forts at Borstal, Bridgewoods,

Horsted and Luton. All four were built on higher ground to the south of Rochester and Chatham, the concrete structures disguised with rubble and grass to make them look like hillocks. Subsequently two redoubts were built to the east at Twydall in Gillingham and the circle was completed in 1899 with the building of another fort at Darland to the south-east. The forts were the last of their kind to be built in this country and their defensive potential was never tested.[11]

Cement, Engineering and Barge-building

The fortunes of the cement and brick industries in the lower Medway valley were closely linked to the fluctuations in demand for building materials in London. Both industries expanded rapidly in the 1870s as London experienced a building boom and slumped as the market for new housing entered a period of depression in the late 1880s. The transport of finished products to London by water also stimulated the local barge-building trade and engineering works. Strood had at least three successful engineering companies in the latter half of the 19th century: the Eagle Iron works, Collis & Stace and the largest, Aveling & Porter.[12]

Aveling & Porter

Thomas Aveling had begun his career repairing agricultural machinery in a small works in Rochester, but his business expanded and he developed, among other things, the steam traction engine. He moved his growing business to Strood in 1861 and brought additional capital into the company by forming a partnership with Richard Porter in 1862. That year the inhabitants of Chatham and Rochester were treated to a demonstration of the power of his new machinery when a 10-horsepower engine

Figure 93 The Aveling & Porter works were situated on the riverside at Strood to the south of Rochester Bridge. What remained of these buildings was demolished in 2010, despite a local campaign to preserve this part of the area's industrial heritage.

dragged a load of 21 tons on five carriages 'up Star Hill, along the New Road to the Station, returning through the narrow streets of Chatham with the greatest facility'. The purpose of this demonstration was to show visiting 'foreigners of distinction' and future customers the potential of the new engines. According to the local paper they were 'much astonished at the rate with which the heavy mass moved up and down hill and the manner in which the long train turned the sharp corners of streets'. Despite initial concerns about the damage these vehicles might cause to the roads, the popularity of road steam locomotive engines grew and their manufacture continued at the Strood works until the 1920s alongside the production of steam rollers, tram engines and cement-making machinery. By the end of the 19th century the company provided work for around 1,000 men.[13]

Another important engineering company set up shop in the Medway Towns just before the First World War. The aircraft manufacturers Short Bros were already manufacturing aircraft at Eastchurch on the Isle of Sheppey. In 1913 the firm moved to the Rochester riverside, south of the bridge, to be close to the smooth, sheltered water that they needed to test their latest innovation, the seaplane.[14]

The Decline of the Fishing Industry

Fishing, a traditional industry on the tidal stretches of the river Medway, was in decline by the 1860s and had all but disappeared by 1910. The oyster fishery struggled after a series of hard winters which killed off the stock and despite the Rochester Oyster Fishery Act of 1865, which aimed to improve the position of the oyster fishermen and their trade, other factors continued to mitigate against a revival of the industry. The extension of Chatham Dockyard in the 1860s resulted in the closure of creeks around St Mary's Island and river embankments were built. These activities, necessary for the construction and safety of the dockyard, reduced the territory of the oyster fishery. At the same time, the river was becoming increasingly polluted with sewage and industrial waste from local manufacturing industries. The 1881 census for Strood recorded not a single dredgerman or oyster fisherman and by 1914 there were only a handful of boats and 20 dredgermen employed in oyster fishing in the estuary where 50 years earlier the industry had employed 400. At this time the town clerk of Rochester noted that 'The Oyster Fishery used to be a very large affair, but it fell on hard times.'[15]

Other forms of fishing fared slightly better but still went into decline from the 1860s. A statement by a local councillor, reported

in the local paper, suggested that the fishermen were in part to
blame as they had overfished the local shrimps, sole and plaice that
formed the bulk of the catch. In Councillor Boucher's opinion, 'the
fishery ... was conducted in such a manner as not only to reflect
discredit on the city but also to do injury to the community at
large'. The autumn catches of herring also declined from the 1870s.
The extent of the changes in local industry is evident from the
census return for Strood for 1881, in which there were nearly twice
as many men employed in the cement industry (73) as fishermen
(40). By 1910 there were just 21 boats and 52 men from the four
Medway Towns who fished regularly in the estuary.[16]

POPULATION GROWTH

These changes in the local economy had a significant effect on the
population of the Medway Towns. Although the rate of growth
fluctuated, the number of people living in the four Medway towns
more than doubled in the second half of the 19th century. There
was a period of rapid increase between 1851 and 1871, followed
by a decade of stagnation, then growth picked up again from 1881
to the end of the century. Although the population of all four
towns grew, the rate of increase was different in each, reflecting
the differing demands of local industry. Rochester, least affected by
industrial growth, saw the least dramatic change – its population
grew steadily over the period, increasing by just over 50 per cent to
around 17,000 by the end of the century. Strood, the smallest of the
four, benefitted from the expansion of the cement and engineering
industries and more than trebled its population, from 3,000 in
1851 to about 10,500 in 1901. Chatham, with the largest population
in 1851, continued to increase throughout the period but was

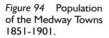

Figure 94 Population
of the Medway Towns
1851-1901.

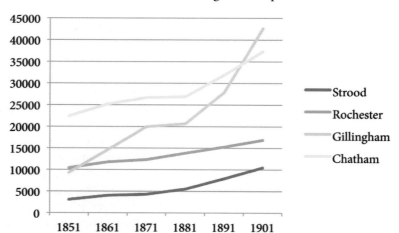

outstripped by Gillingham by 1891 and remained in second place through to the end of the century. Gillingham, home to most of the new dockyard workforce, experienced the most rapid growth of all. From a starting point of just over 9,000 in 1851, the population had doubled by 1881 and doubled again to reach 42,643 by 1901. As the Medway Towns entered the 20th century, 40 per cent of its inhabitants lived in Gillingham.

Migration

Where did all these people come from? The level of population increase in the Medway Towns can only be accounted for by increased levels of migration. An analysis of the 1871 census shows that most of the first wave of new inhabitants of Gillingham who worked in Chatham Dockyard had come to the area from outside the Medway Towns. Like the immigrants of the 1850s and '60s, the skilled workers such as shipwrights came from other dockyard and coastal towns from all over the United Kingdom. This included a significant number from London, prompted to move for work, following the closure of the Deptford and Woolwich shipyards in 1869. In contrast, most of the unskilled labourers came not from coastal towns but from agricultural communities in the Home Counties seeking better prospects and hoping for more regular employment in Chatham Dockyard.[17]

New Communities

The impact of this rapid population growth on the built environment of the Medway Towns is still very much in evidence today. Row upon row of Victorian terraced houses stretch up the steep hillsides that surround Chatham town centre, and the area between Gillingham railway station and the old town centre is crammed full of housing built as the population exploded in the late 19th century. The process of filling in every available space began in earnest in the second half of the 19th century.

The first phase of development was the 'mushroom town' of New Brompton. This had begun to grow in the 1850s on the farmland between the Lines and the original village of Gillingham. By the 1890s a whole new community was established between the eastern end of the extended dockyard and the railway line and continued to spread between the railway and the main Dover to London Road (later the A2) in the early years of the 20th century.

The new town had something of a frontier feel to it in the early days. Indeed a letter to the *Chatham News* in 1868 complained of bad language and fighting on the streets, 'which would make anyone think he was walking through some Californian gold diggings'. This was perhaps an exaggeration in an area which by the 1870s had its own church, at least four nonconformist chapels and National and Wesleyan schools, but it did take some time for the new residents to work together in harmony for the improvement of their locality. Although the ratepayers agreed to pay for gas lighting for the streets, the cleaning and maintenance of roads was left to individual householders as the idea of a Board of Health to oversee this task was rejected by ratepayers on the grounds of cost. As a consequence, according to another correspondent to the local paper, the streets were 'allowed to remain like ploughed fields which cannot be crossed in wet weather without sinking ankle deep in mud'. He further complained of 'a mountain of horse and pig dung' from stables and pig sties in close proximity to houses and a well. Serious outbreaks of smallpox and cholera in the area in the early 1870s raised alarm bells and the formation in 1873 of the Gillingham Board of Health marked the beginning of an improvement in the condition of the streets and the quality of the water supply.[18]

Another of the more encouraging signs for the well-being of the local community was the formation in 1867 of the New Brompton Economical Provisions Society. The increasing cost of buying meat prompted a group of dockyard workers to band together for the purpose of bulk purchasing what was regarded as an essential foodstuff. Within the first year they managed to negotiate a 30 per cent reduction in the price of mutton, and soon branched out into the provision of general foodstuffs. By 1877 they had acquired premises and it was estimated that they were able to save members

Figure 95 New Brompton High Street in the early 1900s, a thriving commercial centre supplying the rapidly increasing population of the area. A new electric tram service was introduced in 1902.

4s. 6d. in the pound (22.5 per cent) on food purchases. This local organisation eventually became part of the national Co-operative Society movement.[19]

The expansion of Chatham and Rochester was less dramatic. Building on the higher ground to the south of the towns was severely restricted by the army's ownership of the land on which the forts had been built to protect the dockyard. The centre of Chatham was already crowded and housing began to straggle along the road toward the village of Luton. This area was less attractive to dockyard workers, being too far from the yards for an easy journey to work. This changed in 1902 when a tramline offering a 15-minute ride from Luton to the yard gates was introduced and Luton began to be transformed from a quiet rural village to a busy suburb of Chatham.

POLITICAL CHANGE

Incorporation for all

As Chatham and Gillingham continued to grow in the second half of the century, the question once again arose of whether those towns should seek to establish a more appropriate form of local government for themselves. The Municipal Corporations Act of 1835 had given towns the right to petition for incorporation. That option, quickly taken up by many of the industrial towns of the north, had been considered and rejected by Chatham and Gillingham in the 1830s but they reconsidered it later. A notice appeared in the *Chatham News* of 31 July 1861 calling a public meeting to discuss incorporation on the grounds that:

> the progress, importance and commercial prosperity of our town are not moving onwards as might be expected in a town like Chatham, and as we are not in possession of all the powers of local self government that a town of so much importance should enjoy …

A meeting was held and a committee of 15 was formed with 10 members from Chatham and five representing Brompton and New Brompton. Once again the initiative failed. Within a week the Brompton representatives had withdrawn on the grounds that they felt incorporation was too expensive. Although discussions continued among those from Chatham, at a public meeting in September of the same year the majority voted against incorporation and the idea was shelved.[20]

Although no agreement could be reached then regarding the local government of Gillingham and Chatham, a few years later a national initiative had its effect on the political landscape of both towns. An investigation prompted by the Representation of the People Act of 1867 came to the conclusion that the electoral boundaries of the Chatham constituency should be extended to include the parish of Gillingham. The towns shared a member of parliament as well as their economic reliance on Chatham Dockyard, but these common interests made little difference. When a further attempt was made to revive the idea of incorporation in 1877, the instigators were thwarted at an early stage by local objections.[21]

While Chatham and Gillingham failed to reach agreement on the matter of local government, relationships between Chatham and Rochester continued to be uncomfortable. An editorial in the *Chatham News* in 1876 used the occasion of the opening of a skating rink in Chatham to comment on this state of affairs:

> Here at last will be a neutral ground where the 'Rochester gentlemen' may meet the 'Chatham gentlemen' without coming into collision, – if they will all but go in the same direction and use their skates deftly, but when did Rochester and Chatham go harmoniously and smoothly together, except at public dinners, where social and complimentary 'butter' liberally dealt out has such a lubricating effect.[22]

Yet another national initiative brought matters to a head again in the following decade. The Local Government Act of 1888 offered the opportunity for large conurbations, such as that formed by the Medway Towns, to become county boroughs with extensive powers over local finances and administration. The local press campaigned strongly for this change, arguing that the Medway Towns were not properly represented by Kent County Council, whose concerns were overwhelmingly rural. A committee led by Sir John Gorst, MP for Chatham and Gillingham, was set up in May 1888 and discussions began between representatives from Chatham and Gillingham. Rochester, although invited to the table, remained aloof, fearing that the genteel community would be overwhelmed by its more populous and rowdy neighbours.

Once again the discussions between Gillingham and Chatham ended in disagreement. Gillingham wanted equal representation within the proposed county borough, which Chatham was not prepared to grant. The location of the town hall also became a bone of contention. By the beginning of August all thoughts

Figure 96 The coat of arms created for the newly formed borough of Gillingham in 1903, with the motto 'With fort and fleet for home and England'.

of joint action had been abandoned. Gillingham backed out and Chatham considered seeking incorporation on its own, the proponents of this plan declaring openly, 'we want a Mayor and Corporation to balance us against the position of Rochester.'[23]

The proposal for Chatham to go ahead on its own met with general approval in the local community. A public meeting and subsequent petition concluded that:

> it is generally felt that the grant of a charter would tend to the better government of and import dignity and importance to the town, give an impetus to trade and create a greater interest in the conduct of public affairs among business men and thereby promote the welfare of the inhabitants.[24]

An official enquiry followed and incorporation was granted on 22 November 1890, with a grand public celebration on 10 December 1890.[25]

Gillingham inched towards incorporation during the final decade of the 19th century. A local Board of Health had been created in 1873, administering roads, water and sewage. In 1894 an act to make the town an Urban District Council came into force. This was only a partial step towards political modernisation as this new body administered local affairs in parallel with the ancient court leet until borough status was finally achieved in 1903. The driving force behind the incorporation of Gillingham was Charles Smith, a local draper who had also played a significant role in the incorporation of Chatham and had been mayor there from 1891-3.

When Gillingham's charter of incorporation was issued in 1903, it was an occasion for ceremony and celebration, as it had been for Chatham 13 years before. On 9 September the charter was collected by local dignitaries from the office of the Privy Council in London and, on return to the town, was read aloud in four locations. A souvenir booklet was issued recording the events of the day, including the provision of tea and cakes for the schoolchildren.

THE FACE OF THE INCORPORATED TOWNS

It was not only new housing that changed the face of the Medway Towns. With incorporation came a desire for municipal buildings to reflect this new political status and house the employees of the corporation. Chatham town hall, completed in 1900, was a typical late Victorian council building, its grandeur symbolic of the newly established town council's influence in the local area. In similar vein was the building of a new free public library on New Road.

Figure 97 Chatham
Town Hall not long
after its completion in
1899 to designs by a
local architect, George
E. Bond. It represented a
considerable investment
for the newly formed
borough council who
clearly aimed at a
fashionable design.

Figure 98   The Chatham
Free Library on New
Road was built at the turn
of the 20th century in a
more progressive style
than the Town Hall. It has
been demolished.

Churches and chapels

The increased population also required new places of worship which made new landmarks in the local community. As mentioned in panel 4, New Brompton soon had several churches and chapels to meet the needs of worshippers, and others were built throughout the Medway Towns during the late 19th century. The most striking of these, although the least used, was Jezreel's tower. Located in Gillingham at the highest point of Chatham Hill, the building was commissioned by the self-proclaimed leader of the Jezreelite sect,

Figure 99 Jezreel's Tower, Gillingham, headquarters of the Jezreelites, a local sect founded by a former soldier, James Roland White, later known as James Jershom Jezreel. Begun in 1886 on the top of Chatham Hill, this four-square building based on Revelation xxi: 16 was to be surrounded by shops run by the tradesmen members of the congregation as well as accommodation for Israel's International College. Never completed, the tower was demolished in 1961.

James Jershom Jezreel, a former soldier based in Chatham. The tower was to be the headquarters of the sect. Jezreel died before the work began and although the project was started by his widow in 1886 she too died in 1888. The sect, which at one point had more than 1,400 followers in Chatham and Gillingham, declined rapidly following Jezreel's death and the work was never completed. The tower stood in its unfinished state until demolition in 1961.[26]

Leisure and Pleasure

Theatres

Increased leisure and a booming economy also brought a demand for new places of entertainment. Theatre and music hall were increasingly popular in late 19th-century England. Rochester had had a small theatre since the late 18th century, but first Chatham and then Gillingham offered a good night out at the

Figure 100 The Grand Theatre in Skinner Street, Gillingham, photographed in 1920. It opened as a theatre in 1910 and was converted to a cinema shortly afterwards.

theatre for their resident working population. Chatham boasted one of the earliest music halls in the country with its Palace of Varieties. Established in 1847 next to the *Railway Tavern* at the west end of Chatham High Street, the theatre burned down in 1879 but was rebuilt on a grander scale and opened in July 1886 as Barnard's New Palace of Varieties. The Barnard family were also responsible for the Theatre Royal on the corner of the High Street and Manor Road. It opened in 1899 and seated around three thousand. Badly damaged by fire the following year, it reopened in December 1900.[27]

Figure 101 The Theatre Royal, Chatham, contemporary with the Town Hall and by the same architect, G.E. Bond. He gave it a huge auditorium behind a narrow façade in the baroque style then popular for theatres and music halls. Closed in the 1950s, the theatre was demolished in 2009.

In Gillingham local entertainment also began in a pub with the Gaiety Music Hall being advertised as operating in the *Shepherd and Shepherdess* pub on Wood Street, Brompton. By the early years of the 20th century there were several theatres in New Brompton. The largest of these was the Grand on Skinner Street, which opened in 1910, seating 800 and was converted into a cinema shortly afterwards. The Hippodrome also went through several incarnations, starting out in 1904 as a 'prefab' to house circuses; it too was later used as a cinema and then a roller-skating rink.[28]

Pubs and brothels

The pubs continued to do a roaring trade, a matter of particular concern in Chatham, which had to deal with crowds of thirsty soldiers, sailors and dockworkers. Concern was translated into the provision of missions and rest homes in an attempt to provide alternative alcohol-free and morally uplifting entertainment for the armed forces.

More successful in providing entertainment for this client group were the pubs and brothels of Chatham. Prostitution was perceived as a major problem in port towns and near to military bases and Chatham was notorious for its prostitute population,

centred around the Brook. The town was one of those for whom
the Contagious Diseases Acts of the 1860s were conceived in
an attempt to curb the practice of prostitution and to prevent
the spread of venereal disease. A doctor visiting Chatham in
1867 to investigate the effects of the act noted that in Chatham
and Sheerness 'about 260 women are under surveillance. This
number includes only notorious prostitutes. There are, besides
them, many factory workers, servant girls and married women,
who practice prostitution clandestinely.' A letter to the *Chatham
Observer* the following year complained angrily of the 'filthy
vile language' of the prostitutes on the streets of Chatham
and the fights provoked by drunken soldiers. The problem of
drunkenness escalated over the following two decades, often
erupting into violence that the Chatham police were unable
to control.[29]

A serious problem for the local police was that they were
undermanned. Chatham did not have its own force but drew
its police from the Kent County constabulary. In 1871 the town
was allocated only one police inspector and 12 constables for
a population of over 26,000. The situation was made worse
by the superior policing enjoyed by neighbouring Rochester.
Here the city corporation could raise its own police force
under the control of a chief constable who had a force of 28
men for a population half the size of Chatham. The situation
did not improve until 1885 when there was a 30 per cent
increase in the number of constables allocated to Chatham and
Gillingham from the county constabulary. This improvement
was achieved largely by the efforts of three men, George
Winch, George Church and Adam Stignant, the latter said to
have been perceived by contemporaries as 'the uncrowned
king of Chatham'. The three men, all members of the local
Board of Health, also took a leading role in the move for the
incorporation of Chatham in the 1880s.[30]

Sport
A more positive aspect of the presence of the military in the area
was their promotion of sport, particularly football and yachting.
The Royal Engineers had a successful football team from the 1850s.
In 1893 a professional team was formed in the Medway Towns with
the backing of a group of local businessmen who bought the land
on which the stadium of Gillingham FC stands today. Known as
New Brompton FC until 1913, when it was renamed Gillingham,
the team joined the second division of the Southern League in
1894. They finished top of the division in the 1894-5 season and
gained promotion to the First Division where they remained until

the suspension of the Football League on the outbreak of the First World War.

The growth of industry in the lower Medway area brought a new moneyed class that popularised water sports to the area. Again the Royal Engineers had taken the lead in this leisure activity and had established a rowing club in the late 1840s. This was soon expanded to include yachting, and a clubhouse was built near Gillingham fort in 1859. Membership was limited to army men and it was not until 1879 that the Medway Yacht Club was formed. By the end of the 19th century sailing as a sport was firmly established on the lower Medway with annual regattas and regular races. Another facet of boat racing on the river was the annual barge race. Friendly rivalry between barge owners on the Thames and the Medway had led to the first race on the Thames in 1863, and in 1880 the first Medway barge race was held.[31]

By 1914 all four of the Medway Towns were truly urban in character. Much of the previously undeveloped land on the riverbanks had been taken over by industrial development, and agriculture and fishing was in decline. Many new workers came to the area, drawn by the increasing opportunities for employment offered by the expansion of Chatham Dockyard, the boom in cement manufacture and in engineering. This influx of people needed housing, prompting the development of New Brompton and Luton. With the expansion of the towns the benefits of improved political status were achieved. Both Chatham and Gillingham achieved incorporation, placing them on an equal footing with Rochester in terms of local government.

There were problems. River and air pollution, poor sanitation, fluctuating economic fortunes, all impacted on the physical and social environment of the towns and political change had only been achieved with considerable wrangling. But the late 19th and early 20th centuries also saw positive changes in the towns. Chatham Dockyard continued to adapt to the changing requirements of the Royal Navy, new industries brought wealth to the towns, improved civic and leisure facilities became available, new housing was built. Overall the Medway Towns had gained from the previous hundred years and entered the 20th century in a more stable position, economically, politically and socially.

AFTERWORD

In 1550 there was only one settlement at the mouth of the river Medway that could claim to be a town. Rochester, ancient cathedral city and the proud possessor of a borough charter, reigned supreme. As the preceding chapters have shown, the overwintering of the English fleet at Chatham in the mid-16th century began a process which altered the balance of power between the communities on the banks of the Medway and by the early 20th century all four communities could legitimately claim to be towns. Although Rochester was still the jewel in the crown of the Medway Towns in terms of its historic architecture and cultural superiority, it no longer dominated economically or politically. First Chatham, then Gillingham had expanded to meet the demands of Chatham Dockyard and during the course of the 19th century Strood was transformed from a busy fishing community to an industrial town reliant on cement and engineering.

All of these aspects of life in the Medway Towns were a consequence of the position of these communities on the banks of the river Medway. Rochester grew from a crossing point on the river. The port of Rochester was ideally placed on the river to control the movement of goods in and out of the estuary. The riverbanks of the parishes of Chatham and Gillingham offered a good berth for the Royal Navy and an ideal location for shipbuilding and repair. Strood made its living first from the oysters and fish in the river and then by using the river to export the bricks and cement made from natural resources found on the riverbanks.

These natural advantages were enhanced by the towns' proximity to London, which was easily accessible by road and sea. Oversight of Chatham Dockyard was maintained by the Admiralty, based in the capital but with local representation in the yards. London's population growth stimulated the economy of the Medway Towns, boosting agriculture in the area in the 16th and 17th centuries by increased demands for food, and the successive building booms of the 19th century stimulated the cement and brick industries on the river Medway. Natural resources, agricultural produce and manufactured goods could be easily and swiftly sent to the markets and building sites of the capital and this advantage was exploited to the full in the second half of the 19th century.

The past of the four communities can be clearly traced in the Medway Towns today. The cathedral, bridge and castle still dominate the skyline of Rochester, the riverbanks of Gillingham and Chatham are still home to the dockyard and the hillsides of all four towns are densely covered in 19th-century housing. The evidence of the past still has a major part to play in the local economy. Although no ships have been built in Chatham Dockyard since its closure in 1984, the site is now an important centre for the tourism and leisure industries and the historic buildings of Rochester are appreciated more by tourists today than by 19th-century visitors. The open spaces that formed the Great Lines military defences have become a park for the locals and visitors to enjoy, and many of the houses built for the influx of 19th-century dockyard and engineering workers provide homes for those who commute daily to London for work

The river Medway, too, has found a new role in the 21st century. With the loss of shipbuilding and manufacturing industries on the riverbanks, the river has become an important part of the leisure industry. Water quality has improved dramatically in the past thirty years and fishing, once a means of making a living for many, has enjoyed a revival as a popular leisure activity, along with sailing and cruising the river on the *Kingswear Castle*, the last surviving paddle-steamer. The barge races begun by barge manufacturers in the late 19th century are still keenly fought today.

The river Medway and Chatham Dockyard continue to be integral to life in the Medway Towns as they have been for over five hundred years. Visitors today are just as impressed by the sight of river and dockyard as Lambarde and Defoe before them.

Endnotes

INTRODUCTION

1 W. Lambarde, *A perambulation of Kent* (1596 edn, reprinted Bath, 1970), 310.

CHAPTER 1   The Arrival of the Dockyards, 1550-1580

1 C. Young, 'The Physical Setting', in T. Lawson and D. Killingray (eds), *An Historical Atlas of Kent* (2004), 1-6.

2 http://www.nottingham.ac.uk/english/ins/kepn/detailpop.php?placeno=2628 [accessed 9 March 2009].

3 G.J. Copley (ed.), *Camden's Britannia: Kent* (1977), 28.

4 Copley, *Camden*, 29.

5 F. Cull, 'Chatham dockyard: early leases and conveyances for its building during the 16th and 17th centuries', *Archaeologica Cantiana* LXXIII (1959), 76-7.

6 P. MacDougall, *The Chatham Dockyard Story* (Rochester, 1981), 10-11; Cull, 'Chatham dockyard', 77.

7 MacDougall, *Chatham Dockyard*, 16-18. R. Baldwin, *The Gillingham Chronicles* (Rochester, 1989), 79.

8 W. Lambarde, *A perambulation of Kent* (reprinted Bath, 1970, first published 1596), 311-13.

9 E. Hasted, 'The city and liberty of Rochester: General history and description', *The History and Topographical Survey of the County of Kent*, Vol. 4 (1798), 45-86; http://www.british-history.ac.uk/report.aspx?compid=53798 [accessed 13 March 2009].

10 M.E. Mate, *Trade and Economic developments 1450-1550: The experience of Kent, Surrey and Sussex* (2006), 239. A multiplier of six is applied to the number of taxpayers in the 1522 lay subsidy. J.M. Gibson, 'The 1566 survey of the Kent coast', *Archaeologica Cantiana*, CXII (1993) 341-53. A multiplier of five is applied to the number of households. M. Zell, *Early Modern Kent 1640-1740* (2000), 144-5, suggests that this may be an underestimate of the total population. C. Chalklin, *Seventeenth-century Kent* (1965), 30-3; as Rochester had about 3,000 inhabitants in 1664, it is unlikely that there were less than 1,500 in the mid-16th century.

11 P. Clarke and P. Slack, *English Towns in Transition 1500-1700* (1976), 4.

12 For details of all the city charters and boundaries see F.F. Smith, *A History of Rochester* (first published 1928, reprinted Chatham 1976), 39-62.

13 Smith, *Rochester*, 236-7.

14 Mate, *Trade and Economic Developments 1450-1550*, 40-2.

15 Smith, *Rochester*, 210.

16 Smith, *Rochester*, 218.

17 Smith, *Rochester*, 220.

18 J.M. Gibson, 'The 1566 survey of the Kent coast', *Archaeologica Cantiana*, CXII (1993), 341-53

19 J.M. Gibson, 'Rochester Bridge, 1530-1660', in N. Yates and J.M. Gibson (eds), *Traffic and Politics: the Construction and Management of Rochester Bridge, AD43-1993* (1994), 107-60.

20 Gibson, 'Rochester Bridge', 121.

21 MacDougall, *Chatham Dockyard*, 16.

22 C.S. Knighton, 'The reformed chapter, 1540-1660', in N. Yates (ed.), *Faith and Fabric: A History of Rochester Cathedral, 604-1994* (1996), 57-68.

23 P. Mussett, 'The reconstituted chapter, 1660-1820', in Yates, *Faith*, 95. Knighton, 'Reformed', in Yates, *Faith*, 68.

24 S.E. Rigold, *Temple Manor, Strood, Rochester, Kent* (English Heritage), 1990; http://www.english-heritage.org.uk/daysout/properties/temple-manor-history-and-research/ [accessed 3 October 2011].

25 MacDougall, *Chatham Dockyard*, 10. MALSC P85/1/1, Parish Register Chatham St Mary 1568-1614; P153/1/1, Parish Register, St Mary Magdalene, Gillingham, 1568-1651; P150B/1/1, Parish Register, St Nicholas, Strood 1565-1639.
26 MALSC, P85/1/1, Parish Register Chatham St Mary 1568-1614.
27 A.F. Pollard, *Tudor Tracts* (1964), 229-30, quoting from 'The History of Wyat's rebellion: with the order and manner of resisting the same' (1555).
28 H. Plomer, 'The Churchwarden's accounts for St Nicholas at Strood, Part 1, 1555-1600' *Kent Archaeological Society Record Series,* Vol. V (1927), 9.
29 J.G. Coad, *Historic architecture of the Royal Navy* (1983), 19-20.

CHAPTER 2   A Home for the Fleet, 1580-1640
 1 P. MacDougall, *The Chatham Dockyard Story* (Rochester, 1981), 21-2.
 2 TNA, AO1788/323.
 3 F. Cull, 'Chatham Dockyard: early leases and conveyances for its building during the 16th and 17th centuries', *Archaeologica Cantiana*, LXXIII (1958), 81.
 4 SA, D593/S/4, W. Borough to William Lambarde, 26 October 1595.
 5 MacDougall, *Chatham Dockyard*, 23-4, quoting Lord Howard to Lord Burghley, 1588.
 6 C. Chalklin, *Seventeenth-Century Kent* (1965), 141.
 7 J. Andrews, 'Industries in Kent, *c.*1500-1640', in M. Zell (ed.), *Early Modern Kent 1540-1640* (2000), 125-6.
 8 M. Oppenheim (ed.), 'The Naval Tracts of Sir William Monson', *Navy Records Society,* Vol. XLVII (1914), 4-15.
 9 W.G. Perrin (ed.), 'The autobiography of Phineas Pett', *Navy Records Society* (1917), 6, lv-lxiv & 63; MacDougall, *Chatham Dockyard,* 29-33.
10 Cull, 'Chatham Dockyard', 81-2.
11 F. Cull, 'Chatham – The Hill House (1567-1805)', *Archaeologica Cantiana*, LXXVII (1962), 95, 97; Perrin, 'Phineas Pett', 2.
12 MacDougall, *Chatham Dockyard*, 30-2.
13 SA, D593/S/4/37/2, W. Borough to William Lambarde, 26 October 1595. MALSC, P85, Chatham St Mary 1568-1974; P153, Gillingham, St Mary Magdelen, 1558-1967.
14 SA D593/S/4/14/12, list of farmers in Chatham, Gillingham, Isle of Grain possessing grain stocks, 1596; SA D593/S/4/14/13, list of householders needing corn in Gillingham and Chatham, 1596.
15 P. Clark, *English Provincial Society* (1977), 247, quoting from J. Strype, *Annals of the Reformation* (Oxford, 1824), IV, 315-16.
16 CKS, QM/SIq/26 18 March 1604/5, QM/SIq/27, 18 March 1604/5; Paul Hastings, 'Radical movements and worker's protests to *c.*1850', in F. Lansberry (ed.), *Government and politics in Kent, 1640-1914* (2001), 95-6. See also P. Clarke 'Popular protest and disturbance in Kent, 1558-1640', *Economic History Review,* 2nd series, XXIX, 3 (1976), 365-82.
17 MacDougall, *Chatham Dockyard*, 31-2; P. MacDougall, 'Industrial Disputes in Chatham Dockyard', *Bygone Kent*, Vol. 1, 5 (May 1980), 266.
18 J.D. Crawshaw, *The history of Chatham Dockyard* (Newcastle, 1999), 3/5; CSPD, 1627-8, Vol. XLIX, 21.
19 M. Blatcher, 'Chatham Dockyard and a little known shipwright, Matthew Baker 1530-1613', *Archaeologica Cantiana*, CVII (1989),166-7.
20 N. Yates and J. Gibson, *Traffic and Politics: the construction and management of Rochester Bridge, AD 43-1993)*, 293.
21 MALSC, DRc Els 1.
22 MALSC, U398/M5, records of the Manor of Twydall in Gillingham.
23 For details of all the city charters and boundaries see F.F. Smith, *A History of Rochester* (first published 1928, reprinted Chatham 1976), 39-62.
24 SA D593/S/4/55/1/3.
25 Thanks are due to Catherina Clement for her generosity in sharing this both this information and the following references extracted from the records of Rochester City Council
26 MALSC, Rochester City Customal, MTC/MR/105 ff 83b-84b, 113a-b; Smith, *Rochester,* 495-6, 77. MALSC, Rochester City Customal, MTC/MR/105 ff54b, 75b, RCA/A1/1 ff321, 359, 505.

27 Smith, *Rochester,* 77.

28 CSPD 1634-5, Vol. 285.

29 SA D593/S/4/14/12, list of farmers in Chatham, Gillingham, Isle of Grain possessing grain stocks, 1596. TNA Prob. 11/163, Will of John Punnett, fisherman of Strood, proved 23 Feb 1632.

30 MALSC, U398/M5 Manor of Twydall in Gillingham.

31 MALSC, U398/M5 Manor of Twydall in Gillingham.

CHAPTER 3   Destruction, disease and the Dutch invasion, 1640-1680

1 A. Everitt, *The community of Kent and the great rebellion, 1640-60* (Leicester, 1966); J. Eales, 'Kent and the English Civil Wars. 1640-1660', in F. Lansberry (ed.), *Governments and politics in Kent, 1640-1914* (2001).

2 P. MacDougall, *The Chatham Dockyard Story* (1981), 34; Eales, 'Kent and the English Civil Wars', 1-3.

3 *A perfect diurnall of the severall passages in our late journey into Kent* (1642), 2-4; CSPD 1641-3, 374-5.

4 Quoted in Everitt, *The community of Kent,* 113.

5 *Mercurius Rusticus* (London 1643, reprinted 1971), 155-6, quoted in C.S. Knighton, 'The Reformed Chapter 1540-1600', in N. Yates (ed.), *Faith and Fabric: a history of Rochester Cathedral 604-1994* (1996), 76.

6 P. Mussett, 'The reconstituted chapter, 1660-1820', in Yates, *Faith and Fabric,* 77. Knighton, 'Reformed Chapter', 76.

7 H. Smetham, *History of Strood* (1899), 107, quoting from *First century of scandalous and malignant Priests* (1643).

8 HMC Portland MS Vol. 1, letter Earl of Warwick to Lenthall, 15/11/1643, 152; CSPD 1645-7 336; LJ Vol. 8 9/2/1646 & 14/2/1646.

9 J.R. Powell and E.K. Timmings (eds), 'Documents relating to the Civil War 1642-1648', *Naval Records Society,* (1963), 158; J.B. Hattendorf, R.J. Knight, A.W. Pearsall, N.A. Rodger and G. Till (eds), 'British Naval Documents 1204-1960', *Navy Records Society* (1993),153-5; CSPD 1645-7, 285-6. I am indebted to Catherina Clement for this reference and for much additional assistance given in the preparation of the account of Rochester during the mid-17th century.

10 Letter from Philip Ward to Parliament, 21 May 1648, cited in H. Cary (ed.), *Memorials of the Great Civil War in England from 1646 to 1652,* Vol. 1 (1842), 422-4.

11 Letter Kent County Committee to Parliament, 23 May 1648, cited in C. Firth (ed.), *The Clarke Papers,* Vol. III Camden Series (1899), 16.

12 *Bloudy Newes from Kent Being a Relation of the great Fight at Rochester and Maidstone betwixt the Parliaments army under the command of Lord General Fairfax and the Kentish Forces commanded by Generall Hales London, printed for R W* (1648), 1-3. *Newes from Bowe … Also the particular Relation of the whole businesse in Kent … London printed by E A* (1648), 2, both cited in J. Gibson, 'Rochester Bridge, 1530-1660', in N. Yates and J. Gibson (eds), *Traffic and Politics: the construction and management of Rochester Bridge, AD45-1993,* 156-7.

13 *A letter from Kent of the Rising at Rochester* (1648), 3; Peter Pett to Admiralty Committee, 15 June 1648, 459-62.

14 C. Chalklin, 'Seventeenth-century Kent' (1965), 39.

15 F.F. Smith, *History of Rochester* (1976 edn, first published 1928), 165; M.J. Dobson, *Contours of Death and Disease in Early Modern England* (1997), 408-9.

16 Chalklin, *Kent,* 39; Dobson, *Contours,* 409; Quoted in J. Presnail, *The Story of Chatham* (1976 edn, first published 1952), 123.

17 MacDougall, *Chatham,* 20; MacDougall, *Dockyards,* 65-6.

18 MALSC, P153 Gillingham St Mary Magdalene, 1558-1986.

19 E. Hasted, 'General history: Soil and products', *The History and Topographical Survey of the County of Kent: Volume 1* (1797), 265-71. URL: http://www.british-history. ac.uk/report [accessed 1 August 2008].

20 Dobson, *Contours,* 297.

21 CSPD 1657. *Chatham Observer,* 21 October 1955. Thanks to Odette Buchanan for this reference.

22 MacDougall, *Chatham Dockyard,* 36-7.

23 http://www.pepysdiary.com/archive/1662/08/, http://www.pepysdiary.com/archive/1663/07/, http://www.pepysdiary.com/archive/1663/08/ [accessed 15 October 2009].

24 Presnail, *Chatham,* 122; Macdougall, *Chatham Dockyard,* 40-1.

25 CKS PRS/1/1-25 PRS/I/22/1-4, probate inventory Richard Vaughan, 1668; CKS PRS 1/1/22, probate inventory William Laramer, 1712. See also Dulley, 'People and Homes', 102-3 for similar evidence for Chatham, Rochester and Strood.

26 R. Latham (ed.), *The Illustrated Pepys* (1978), 148. CKS PRS/1/2/110-170, probate inventory, Henry Frewin, 1668.

27 Latham, *Pepys,* 149; Presnail, *Chatham,* 125.

28 Quoted in C.R. Boxer, *The Anglo-Dutch Wars of the 17th century 1652-1674,* (1974), 39.

29 MALSC, P153, Gillingham St Mary Magdalene.

CHAPTER 4   Commercial battles and fine buildings, 1680-1720

1 Celia Fiennes, *Through England on a Side Saddle in the Time of William and Mary* (1702), at http://www.visionofbritain.org.uk/text/chap_page.jsp?t_id=Fiennes&c_id=17 [accessed 4 January 2010].

2 Daniel Defoe, *A tour thro' the whole island of Great Britain* (1727), at http://www.visionofbritain.org.uk/text/chap_page.jsp?t_id=Defoe&c_id=6 [accessed 4 January 2010].

3 D. Harrington (ed.), 'Kent Hearth Tax Assessments Lady Day 1664', *British Records Society Hearth Tax Series,* Vol. 2 (2000).

4 Fiennes, *Through England.*

5 My thanks to Vic Salmon for his invaluable assistance in preparing the following account of the battle for Chatham market. A.F. Dulley, 'Local politics at Rochester, 1710-14', *Archaeologica Cantiana,* LXXIX (1964), 197; P. MacDougall, *Chatham Past* (1998), 38; J. Presnail, *Chatham,* 137.

6 MacDougall, *Chatham Past,* 21-2

7 *Ibid.,* 137.

8 Dulley, 'Local politics', 197-8; Presnail, *Chatham,* 137; CKS, Weller MSS, U38/Z1, 20.

9 CKS, Weller MSS, U38/Z1, 1, 5; Dulley, 'Local politics', 199.

10 Dulley, *ibid.,* 199-201; CKS Weller MSS, U38/Z1, 9.

11 D.C. Coleman, 'Naval Dockyards under the later Stuarts', *Economic History Review,* 2nd series, vi (1953), 136; D. Ormerod, 'Industry, 1640-1800', in A. Armstrong (ed.), *The economy of Kent, 1640-1914',* 103-4; F. Cull, 'Chatham dockyard: early leases and conveyances for its building in the 16th and 17th Centuries', *Archaeologica Cantiana* LXXIII (1960), 85-95; MacDougall, 53; Presnail, *Chatham,* 129-31.

12 MacDougall, *Chatham Past,* 30-1, 56; Celia Fiennes, *Through England.*

13 Defoe, *A tour.*

14 MacDougall, *Chatham Past,* 30-1.

15 F.F. Smith, *A History of Rochester* (1928, reprinted 1976), 65-70.

16 C. Mitchell (ed.), *Hogarth's peregrination* (Oxford, 1962), 5.

17 Smith, *Rochester,* 89-91.

18 Defoe, *A tour.*

19 A.J.F. Dulley, 'People and homes in the Medway Towns 1687-1783', *Archaeologica Cantiana,* LXXVII (1962), 117.

20 S. Burgoyne Black, *A scholar and a gentleman: Edward Hasted, the historian of Kent* (2001), 13-23.

21 The analysis of probate inventories which follows is based on a combination of research done by Dulley in the 1960s published in 'People and homes' and work done for this volume in 2008-9. Dulley's work analysed the records for Rochester, Chatham and Strood in the Rochester Archdeaconry Courts, CKS DRb/Pi 1667/1; 1/1-58/17 and DRa/Pi 1/1-26/9. The work for this volume added the records for Gillingham from the Deanery of Shoreham CKS DRa/Pi. All records are available on microfilm at CKS. Full transcriptions of all 136 Gillingham inventories are available on the EPE Kent website: http://www.englandspastforeveryone.org.uk/Counties/Kent/Explore. Thanks to Pauline Weeds, Margaret Crowhurst, Andrew Ashbee, Pam Doolin and Rebecca Mead for their painstaking work in transcribing these documents.

22 Dulley, 'People and homes', 103. CKS, PRS/1/13/64, William Mitchell, 1709.

23 CKS PRS/1/19/143-169, John Snoborne, 1666.
24 C. Chalklin, *Seventeenth century Kent*, (1965),172-88; Dulley, 'People and homes', 104-6.
25 Dulley, 'People and homes', 106-7
26 *Ibid.*, 108-9
27 CKS PRS/25/1/117, Anthony Woodgate, 1694; PRS/1/14/46, Stephen Simmons, 1711.
28 CKS PRS/1/8/28-34, Richard Hunt, 1668; PRS/1/13/64, William Mitchell, 1709.
29 Harrington (ed.), 'Kent Hearth Tax'.
30 CKS PRS/1/11/17, John King, 1715; PRS/1/2/164 Thomas Burwash, 1705; PRS/1/6/35 Anne Foote, 1710; PRS/1/5/, Crisogen Edridge, 1670; PRS/1/20, Ralph Twisse, 1676.
31 CKS DRb/Pi31/18, John Haywood, 1717; PRS1/15/15, Richard Owen, 1698; CKS PRS/1/19/143-169, Jane Sutton, 1688. See B.A. Holderness, 'Widows in pre-industrial society: an essay upon their economic functions', in R.M. Smith (ed.), *Land, kinship and life-cycle* (Cambridge, 1974), 428, 435. Also M. Hodges, 'Widows of the "middling sort" and their assets in two 17th-century towns'. in T. Arkell, N. Evans and N. Goose, *When death do us part: understanding and interpreting the probate records of early modern England* (Oxford, 2000), 318-21.

CHAPTER 5   Trade, Hurry and Business, 1720-1780

1 A. Saville (ed.), *Secret Comment, the diaries of Gertrude Savile 1721-1757* (Nottingham 1997), 318-19
2 M. Lacy, *The Female Shipwright* (2008 edition, first published 1773); C. Hibbert, *Nelson: a Personal History* (1995), 9-10.
3 E. Hasted, 'Anecdotes of the Hasted family', *Archaeologica Cantiana*, 26 (1904), 277-84. See also S. Burgoyne Black, *A Scholar and a Gentleman: Edward Hasted, the Historian of Kent* (2001), 48-51.
4 P. MacDougall, *Chatham Past* (1999), 38, 47; Saville, *Secret Comment*, 318.
5 Lacy, *Female Shipwright*, 25.
6 TNA ADM/7/660 1773.
7 http://www.hms-victory.com/index.php?option=com_content&task=view&id=71&Itemid=104 [accessed 12 January 2010].
8 Charles Seymour, *A New Topographical, Historical and Commercial Survey of the Cities, Towns and Villages of the County of Kent* (Canterbury, 1776), 237-8.
9 E. Hasted, *The History and Topographical Survey of Kent*, Vol. IV (1798), 194-5.
10 TNA ADM 42/166: ADM 42/172 as quoted in MacDougall, *Chatham Past*, 35. *Ibid.*, 38, 123.
11 B. Ranft, 'Labour relations in the Royal Dockyards in 1739', *Mariners Mirror*, Vol. XLVII, 1961, 286-7; MacDougall, 'The early Industrial dispute: Chatham Dockyard during the 18th century', *Bygone Kent*, Vol. 1, No. 5 (1980), 268.
12 P. MacDougall, 'The early Industrial dispute', 266; Crawshaw, *Chatham Dockyard*, 3/12.
13 MacDougall, *Chatham Dockyard*, 88.
14 *Ibid.*, 89-90.
15 MacDougall, *Chatham Past*, 38-9, 42.
16 This and all subsequent information relating to apprenticeship is from MALSC NF/182/1743-1806, MF/182A 1770-1805. Apprenticeship Records Rochester. Thanks to Astrid Salmon for her transcription of the records and Sally-Ann Ironmonger who entered the data into a spreadsheet for analysis.
17 F.F. Smith, *A history of Rochester* (first printed 1926, reprinted 1976), 208-12.
18 S. Ireland, *Picturesque views on the river Medway* (1793), 51-2.
19 CKS DRb/Pi/42/12, Inventory of James Humphrey, fisherman of Strood.
20 Hasted, *Kent*, Vol. IV, 58; Seymour, *Kent*, 677-8; J.M. Preston, *Industrial Medway: an historical survey* (Rochester, 1977), 32.
21 Seymour, *Kent*, 678.
22 D. Ormrod, 'Rochester Bridge 1660-1825', in N. Yates and J. Gibson (eds), *Traffic and Politics: the construction and management of Rochester Bridge, AD 43-1993* (1994), 167-71.
23 T. Allen, M. Cotterill and G. Pike, *Copperas: an account of the Whitstable works and the first industrial scale chemical production in England* (2004), 30-3.
24 *Ibid.*, 45.

25 Thanks to Vic Salmon for his research on the Best family. P. Mathias, *The Brewing industry in England, 1700-1830* (1959), 198.

26 MALSC U480/F1, Notes on the Best Family; R. Keen, 'Messrs Best, Brewers of Chatham', *Archaeologica Cantiana* (1958), 172-81; *Kentish Post*, 6-20 September 1740. Thanks to Vic Salmon for his assistance in researching the Best Family and their brewing activities.

27 MALSC U480/T170/2 Will of J Mawdistley; A.J. Dulley, 'Local politics at Rochester 1710-14', *Archaeologica Cantiana* (1964), 199.

28 Mathias, *Brewing*, 25; MALSC U480/B572 Cash account; U480/B1 Ledger 1746-54; U480/B802 Rent account.

29 Keen, 'Messrs Best', 172-3. MALSC U480/F20, Bills and estimates.

30 MALSC P85/8/3 Chatham St Mary vestry Minutes 1739-92, 76-8; Hasted, *Kent*, Vol. III, 547.

31 Hasted, *Kent*, Vol. IV, 194.

32 15 & 16 Geo III cap 58 1776.

33 MALSC P85/8/3 Chatham St Mary Vestry Minutes 1739-92, 51-2.

34 Thanks to Odette Buchanan for her research on Caleb Parfect and the Strood workhouse. Extracts are from Caleb Parfect's pamphlet, 'Proposals made in the year 1720, to the Parishioners of Strood in Kent for building a Workhouse there … By the Minister of Strood' (London 1725). Some of this is also reprinted in H. Smetham, *The history of Strood* (1899), 261-87.

35 J. Presnail, *Chatham: the story of a Dockyard town* (Chatham, 1952), 160-1. MALSC U480/P17 Best family of Boxley and Chatham family, estate and business records, contains a plan and elevation of the Chatham Workhouse of 1725. *An Account of Several Work-houses for Employing and Maintaining the Poor* (1732).

36 Seymour, *Kent*, 667-8.

37 Smetham, *Strood*, 217-18.

CHAPTER 6   War, Popular Protest and Fire, 1780-1820

1 John Gale Jones, *A political tour through Rochester, Chatham, Maidstone, Gravesend &c.* (first published 1796, 1997 edn), 17, 33.

2 Jones, *Tour,* 35, 17,19.

3 Jones, *Tour*, 10-11.

4 Hasted, *Kent*, Vol. IV, 194.

5 Hasted, *Kent*, Vol. IV, 58.

6 P. MacDougall, *The Chatham Dockyard Story* (Rochester, 1981), 101-2.

7 *Wrights Topography* (1838), 8.

8 P. MacDougall, *Chatham Past* (1999), 49-50; M. Dobson, 'Population 1640–1831', in A. Armstrong (ed.), *The economy of Kent 1640-1914* (1995), 14.

9 John Byng, *The Torrington Diaries (1784-91),* http://www.visionofbritain.org.uk/text/chap_page.jsp?t_id=Byng&c_id=3 [accessed 2 June 2010]; Jones, *Tour*, 12.

10 Jones, *Tour*, 25-6.

11 William Cobbett, *Rural Rides,* http://www.visionofbritain.org.uk/text/chap_page.jsp?t_id=Cobbett&c_id=3ision [accessed 2 June 2010].

12 MALSC DE402/16/30, a cutting from William Hone, *The Table Book* (1827), 605-6.

13 Jones, *Tour*, 9.

14 MacDougall, *Chatham Dockyard*, 95-7.

15 J. Preston, *Industrial Medway* (Rochester 1977), 19.

16 N. Scarfe, *Innocent espionage: the La Rochefoucauld brother's tour of England in 1785* (Woodbridge, 1995), 230.

17 R. Baldwin, *The Gillingham Chronicles*, 107-11.

18 MacDougal, *Chatham Past*.

19 H. Smetham, *History of Strood* (Rochester, 1899), 55.

20 Baldwin, *Gillingham Chronicles*, 162.

21 Smetham, *Strood*, 249-53.

22 P. MacDougall, 'An Introduction', in Jones, *Political Tour*, i-xi.

23 *Kentish Gazette*, 27, 31 March, 7, 14 April 1795.

24 *Kentish Gazette,* 24 March 1795, MacDougall, 'Introduction', vii.

25 MacDougall 'Introduction', vii-ix; Jones, *Tour*, 37.

26 Jones, *Tour*, 8, 17-18, 26.
27 MALSC RCA/A1/05 Rochester City Council Day Book, April 1787-1812, 58-9. Thanks to Sandra Fowler and Clare Scott for these references.
28 Jones, *Tour*, 6, 13-14.
29 MALSC, DE0414, W. Jeffries, *An account of the fire at Chatham 30 June 1800* (Chatham, 1801), 2.
30 *Ibid.*, 3.

CHAPTER 7   Community life in the Medway Towns, 1820-1860

1 *The European Magazine and London Review*, Vol. 77, 69 (1821); MALSC, DE413, W. Jeffries, *An account of the fire at Chatham in 1820* (Chatham, 1821).
2 *First Report of the Commissioners appointed to enquire into Municipal Corporations in England and Wales* (1835), 859.
3 Samuel Lewis, *A Topographical Dictionary of England*, Vol. 3 (1848), 683; *Wright's Topography of Rochester, Chatham and Strood* (Rochester, 1838), 117-18.
4 Lewis, *A Topographical Dictionary of England* (1848), 250-2; 554-8, http://www.british-history.ac.uk/report.aspx?compid=51315 [accessed 24 June 2010].
5 Tombleson's *The Thames and Medway* (1833-4), 253.
6 Lewis, *A Topographical Dictionary of England* (1848), 291-4, http://www.british-history.ac.uk/report.aspx?compid=50980 [accessed: 24 June 2010].
7 CKS P377/28/33, transcript of journal of Rev.John Woodruff, vicar of Upchurch, 1851-6: 15 April 1852.
8 James Phippen, *Description and sketches of Rochester and district* (1862).
9 M. Waters, *Gleanings from the History of a Dockyard*, 1860-1910, 2. Thanks to Peter Lyons for this reference.
10 T. Denholm, *The Medway Towns 1790-1850; the emergence of Britain's first conurbation* (Rochester, 2001), 19. These figures are from the 1845 Post Office Directory.
11 *Ibid.*, 18-19.
12 R.A. Baldwin, *The Gillingham Chronicles* (Rochester 1998), 193.
13 Thanks are due to Andrew Ashbee and Pam Doolin for their tireless transcription of census data for Strood, Troy Town, Old Brompton and Luton and to David Webb for his assistance in analysing census data for Troy Town and Luton.
14 Baldwin, *Gillingham*, 250, quoting from Henry Coxwell, *My Life and Balloon experiences* (1889).
15 *The Times*, 27 August 1834 and 1 September 1834.
16 MALSC PS/NA/72/11, 1835.
17 MALSC PS/NA/72/6. See also PS/NA/72/9-10.
18 *Maidstone Gazette*, 14 August 1832, MALSC PS/NA/72/8, notice to parish authorities in the Rochester and Gravesend areas 1831; MacDougall, *Chatham Past*, 61-4; C. Collins, KAS Paper no. 004, 'Cholera and Typhoid fever in Kent', http://www.kentarchaeology.ac/authors/004.pdf [accessed 20 October 2010].
19 *Rochester, Chatham & Strood Gazette*, 14 September 1849.
20 MacDougall, *Chatham Past*, 65.
21 MacDougall, *Chatham Dockyard*, 99-103.
22 *Rochester Gazette*, July 1842.
23 J. Preston, *Industrial Medway* (1977), 50-4.
24 Preston, *Industrial Medway*, 57-9; Hann, *Medway Valley*, 23, 45-6.
25 *Chatham News*, 21 July 1860.
26 Preston, *Industrial Medway*, 48-9.
27 T.P. Smith, 'The geographical pattern of coaching services in Kent in 1836', *Archaeologica Cantiana*, XCVIII (1982), 195-9.
28 H. Smetham, *The History of Strood* (Rochester, 1899), 204-6.
29 D. Ormerod, 'Rochester Bridge 1660-1825', in N. Yates and J. Gibson (eds), *Traffic and politics: the construction and management of Rochester Bridge, AD43-1993*, 199-219; J. Preston, 'Rochester Bridge 1825-1950', in Yates and Gibson, *Traffic and Politics*, 221-45.
30 *Illustrated Times*, 24 January 1857, 59.
31 Rochester Corporation Minutes, 18 April 1831 and 25 November 1833, as quoted in I. Jardine, 'The movement for municipal amalgamation in the Medway Towns,

1674-1970' (MA dissertation, University of Kent 1971), 18.

32 *Ibid.*, 19. *Maidstone Gazette & Kentish Courier*, 3 December 1833.

33 'First Report of the Commissioners appointed to enquire into Municipal
     Corporations in England and Wales (1835), 859.

34 Presnail, *Chatham*, 207; Jardine, 'Municipal amalgamation', 26.

35 MacDougall, *Chatham Past*, 58-9.

36 Baldwin, *Gillingham*, 266.

37 MALSC EL/LE/LIM/GM/01/70 1 September 1851.

38 *Environs of London* (1848), quoted in Baldwin, *Gillingham*, 249.

39 *The Times*, 23 July 1849.

CHAPTER 8   Four Towns, 1860-1914

1 C. Dickens, *All the year round* (1893), as quoted in J. Preston, *Industrial Medway; an
    historical survey* (Chatham, 1977), 163.

2 W.L. and M.A. Wylie, *London to the Nore painted and described* (1905), 192;
    A. Munro and P. Row, *Rochester and Chatham with their surroundings, a handbook for
    visitors and residents* (1905), 12.

3 *Chatham, Rochester, Strood & Brompton household almanac and local guide for 1878*
    (Rochester, 1878), passim.

4 G. Phillips Bevan, *Handbook to the County of Kent* (1876), 33-4; *A Handbook for
    travellers in Kent and Sussex* (1868), 90, 92; C. Dickens, *The Uncommercial Traveller*
    (1860): http://www.literaturepage.com/read/dickens-the-uncommercial-traveller-120.
    html [accessed 24 July 2010].

5 P. MacDougall, *The Chatham Dockyard Story* (Rochester,1981), 113-18.

6 *Ibid.*, 117, 123; M. Waters, *Gleanings from the History of a Dockyard, 1860-1910*
    (undated), 6.

7 MacDougall, *Chatham Dockyard*, 104-8, *Rochester Gazette*, 10 September 1862.

8 C. Dickens, *The Uncommercial Traveller* (1860) http://www.online-literature.com/
    view.php/uncommercial-traveller/26 [accessed 16 July 2010].

9 *Chatham News*, August 1908.

10 MacDougal, *Chatham Dockyard*, 127-30.

11 V.T.C. Smith, 'Later nineteenth-century land defences of Chatham', *Post Medieval
     Archaeology*, Vol. 10 (1976), 104-17.

12 Hann, *Medway Valley*, 36-41.

13 *Chatham News,* 30 August 1862. Preston, *Industrial Medway,* 114-24.

14 Preston, *Industrial Medway*, 197-8.

15 R. Goodsall, 'Oyster fisheries on the north Kent coast', *Archaeologica Cantiana*, LXXX
     (1965), 129-30.

16 *Chatham News*, 13 August 1864. E.M. Hewitt, 'Industries', *VCH*, III (1932), 430, 433.

17 Waters, *Gleanings,* 3-4.

18 *Ibid.*, 2.

19 R. Baldwin, *The Gillingham Chronicles* (Rochester, 1998), 254-5

20 I.A.P. Jardine, 'The movement for political amalgamation in the Medway Towns
     1694-1890' (unpublished MA dissertation, University of Kent, 1971), 28-9.

21 *Rochester and Chatham Journal,* 19 May 1877.

22 *Chatham News,* 28 May 1876.

23 *Chatham and Rochester News,* 2 August 1888

24 *Chatham and Rochester News,* 8 September 1888.

25 Jardine, 'Political amalgamation', 30-47.

26 R.A. Baldwin, *The Jezreelites: the rise and fall of a remarkable prophetic movement*
     (Lambarde Press, 1962).

27 MacDougall, *Chatham Past*, 76-7.

28 Baldwin, *Gillingham*, 266-7, 276-8.

29 B. Hill, 'Illustrations of the workings of the contagious diseases act', *British Medical
     Journal* (28 December 1867), 583; MacDougall, *Chatham Past*, 72-3.

30 For a full account of prostitution and policing in 19th-century Chatham, see B. Joyce,
     The Chatham Scandal (Rochester, 1999).

31 Thanks are due to John Basley for the information relating to yachting on the Medway.

Further Reading and Sources

The following is a selective list of the more important sources for the history of the Medway Towns. The books and articles listed below will provide a useful starting point for those wishing to investigate a particular topic further or to investigate topics not covered in this volume.

BOOKS AND ARTICLES

The County of Kent

The following texts are useful to place the Medway Towns in their local and regional context.

Armstrong, A. (ed.), *The economy of Kent, 1640-1914* (1995).

Brandon, P., and Short, B., *The south-east from AD 1000* (1990).

Chalklin, C., *Seventeenth century Kent* (1965).

Clark, P., *English Provincial Society* (1977),

Clarke, P. and Slack, P., *English Towns in Transition 1500-1700* (1976).

Dobson, M.,'Population 1640 – 1831', in A. Armstrong (ed.), *The economy of Kent 1640-1914* (1995).

Clarke, P., 'Popular protest and disturbance in Kent, 1558-1640', *Economic History Review,* 2nd series, XXIX, 3, (1976).

Everitt, A., *The community of Kent and the great rebellion, 1640-60* (1966).

Hann, A., *The Medway Valley: a Kent landscape transformed* (2009).

Lansberry, F. (ed.), *Government and politics in Kent, 1640-1914* (2001)

Lawson, T., and Killingray, D. (eds), *An historical atlas of Kent* (2004).

Palmer, S., 'Kent and the Sea', *Archaeologica Cantiana* CXXVIII (2008).

Zell, M. (ed.), *Early Modern Kent 1640-1740* (2000).

Victoria County History, 3 vols (1932).

The Medway Towns

The following books and articles offer information about specific aspects of life in one or more of the Medway Towns. Many of the topics that have not been covered in this book, for example, education, are included in the studies of individual towns below.

Baldwin, R., *The Gillingham Chronicles* (Rochester, 1989).

Denholm, T., *The Medway Towns 1790-1850; the emergence of Britain's first conurbation* (Rochester, 2001).

Dulley, A.F., 'Local politics at Rochester, 1710-14', *Archaeologica Cantiana*, LXXIX (1964).

Dulley, A.J. 'People and homes in the Medway Towns 1687-1783', *Archaeologica Cantiana*, LXXVII (1962).

Joyce, B., *The Chatham Scandal* (Rochester, 1999).

Joyce, B., *Black People in Medway1655-1914* (Rochester, 2010).

MacDougall, P., *Chatham Past* (1998).

Presnail, J., *Chatham: the story of a Dockyard town* (Chatham, 1976 edn, first published 1952).

Smetham, H., *History of Strood* (1899).

Smith, F.F., *A History of Rochester* (first published 1928, reprinted Chatham 1976).

Yates, N. and Gibson, J.M. (eds), *Traffic and Politics: the Construction and Management of Rochester Bridge, AD43-1993* (1994).

Yates, N. (ed.), *Faith and Fabric: a history of Rochester cathedral, 604-1994* (1996).

The Local Economy

Allen, T., Cotterill, M and Pike, G., *Copperas: an account of the Whitstable works and the first industrial scale chemical production in England* (2004).

Andrews, J., 'Industries in Kent, c.1500-1640', in M. Zell (ed.), *Early Modern Kent 1540-1640* (2000).

Aubry, B., *Red flows the Medway: a labour history of the Medway Towns* (Rochester, 2005).

Banbury, P., *Shipbuilders of the Thames and Medway* (1971).

Coombe, D., *The Bawleymen* (1979).

Gibson, J.M., 'The 1566 survey of the Kent coast', *Archaeologica Cantiana*, CXII (1993)

Goodsall, R., 'Oyster fisheries on the north Kent coast', *Archaeologica Cantiana*, LXXX (1965).

Hastings, P., 'Radical movements and worker's protests to c.1850', in F. Lansberry (ed.), *Government and politics in Kent, 1640-1914* (2001).

Hewitt, E.M., 'Industries', *VCH*, III (1932).

Keen, R., 'Messrs Best, Brewers of Chatham', *Archaeologica Cantiana*, LXXII (1958).

Mate, M.E., *Trade and Economic developments 1450-1550: The experience of Kent, Surrey and Sussex* (2006).

Ormerod, D., 'Industry, 1640-1800', in A. Armstrong (ed.), *The economy of Kent, 1640-1914'* (1995).

Preston, J.M., *Industrial Medway an historical survey* (Rochester, 1977).

Salmon, V., 'James Best, brewer of Chatham, 1744-82', *Cantium*, Vol. 3, 4 (1972).

Smith, T.P., 'The geographical pattern of coaching services in Kent in 1836', *Archaeologica Cantiana*, XCVIII (1982).

Chatham Dockyard, the defences and the military presence.

Blatcher, M., 'Chatham Dockyard and a little known shipwright, Matthew Baker 1530-1613', *Archaeologica Cantiana*, CVII (1989).

Coad, J., *Historic architecture of the Royal Navy* (1983).

Coad, J., *The Royal Dockyards 1690-1850* (1988).

Coleman, D.C., 'Naval Dockyards under the later Stuarts', *Economic History Review*, 2nd series, vi (1953).

Crawshaw, J.D., *The history of Chatham Dockyard* (1999).

Cull, F., 'Chatham – The Hill House (1567-1805)', *Archaeologica Cantiana*, LXXVII (1962).

Cull, F., 'Chatham dockyard: early leases and conveyances for its building during the sixteenth and seventeenth centuries', *Archaeologica Cantiana*, LXXIII (1959).

Douet, J., *British barracks 1600-1914* (1998).

Gulvin, K., *Chatham's concrete ring* (no date).

MacDougall, P., 'Industrial Disputes in Chatham Dockyard', *Bygone Kent*, Vol. 1, 5 (May 1980).

MacDougall, P., 'The early industrial dispute: Chatham Dockyard during the eighteenth century', *Bygone Kent*, Vol. 1, No. 5 (1980).

MacDougall, P., *The Chatham Dockyard Story* (Rochester, 1981).

Ranft, B., 'Labour relations in the Royal Dockyards in 1739', *Mariners Mirror*, Vol. XLVII, (1961).

Smith, V.T.C, 'Later nineteenth-century land defences of Chatham', *Post-Medieval Archaeology*, 10 (1976).

Waters, M., *Gleanings from the History of a Dockyard, 1860-1910* (no date).

Miscellaneous

Aubry, B., *William Cuffay – Medway's Black Chartist* (Rochester 2008).

Baldwin, R.A., *The Jezreelites: the rise and fall of a remarkable prophetic movement* (Lambarde Press, 1962).

Burgoyne Black, S., *A scholar and a gentleman: Edward Hasted, the historian of Kent* (2001).

Collins, C., KAS Paper no. 004 'Cholera and Typhoid fever in Kent. http://www.kentarchaeology.ac/authors/004.pdf..

Copley, G. J. (ed.) *Camden's Britannia: Kent* (1977).

Dobson, M.J., *Contours of Death and Disease in Early Modern England* (1997).

Mathias, P., *The Brewing industry in England, 1700-1830* (1959).

Roake, M. (ed.), *Religious Worship in Kent: the census of 1851* (Maidstone, 1999).

Scarfe, N., *Innocent espionage: the La Rochefoucauld brother's tour of England in 1785* (Woodbridge, 1995).

Yates, N., 'Worship in the cathedral, 1540-1870', in N. Yates (ed.), *Faith and Fabric: a history of Rochester Cathedral 604-1994* (1996).

Yates, W.N., 'The major Kentish towns in the Religious census of 1851', *Archaeologica Cantiana*, 100 (1984).

Unpublished theses

Jardine, I., 'The movement for municipal amalgamation in the Medway Towns, 1674-1970' (MA dissertation, University of Kent, 1971).

Pragnell, H.J., 'The towns of Rochester and Chatham in the eighteenth century: a study in naval administration and social history' (MA dissertation, University of Kent, 1985).

Rees, H. R., 'The Medway Towns – their settlement, growth and economic development' (PhD thesis, University of London, 1954).

PRINTED SOURCES

A Handbook for travellers in Kent and Sussex (1868).

A perfect diurnall of the severall passages in our late journey into Kent, from Aug. 19 to Sept. 3. 1642. By the appointment of both Houses of Parliament. Published for the satisfaction of those who desire true information (1642).

An Account of Several Work-houses for Employing and Maintaining the Poor (1732).

Calendar of State Papers, Domestic (1856-60).

Bruyn Andrews, C., *The Torrington Diaries*, Hon. John Byng, 4 vols (1934).

Cary, H. (ed.), *Memorials of the Great Civil War in England from 1646 to 1652*, Vol. 1 (1842).

Chatham, Rochester Strood & Brompton: household almanac and local guide for 1878 (Rochester, 1878).

Cobbett, W., *Rural Rides* (1830).

Defoe, D., *A tour thro' the whole island of Great Britain* (1727).

Dickens, C., *All the year round* (1893).

Dickens, C., *The Uncommercial Traveller* (1860).

Fiennes, C., *Through England on a Side Saddle in the Time of William and Mary* (1702).

First report of the Commissioners appointed to enquire into Municipal Corporations in England and Wales (1835).

Firth, C. (ed.), *The Clarke Papers*, Vol. III, Camden Series (1899).

Gale Jones, J., *A political tour through Rochester, Chatham, Maidstone, Gravesend &c.* (first published 1796, reprinted, Rochester, 1997).

Harrington, D. (ed.), 'Kent Hearth Tax Assessments Lady Day 1664', *British Records Society Hearth Tax Series*, Vol. 2 (2000).

Harris, J., *History of Kent* (1719).

Hasted, E., 'Anecdotes of the Hasted family', *Archaeologica Cantiana*, 26 (1904).

Hasted, E., *The History and Topographical Survey of the County of Kent*, 2nd edn, 12 vols (Canterbury, 1778-90).

Hattendorf, J.B., Knight, R.J.B., Pearsall, A.W.H., Rodger, N.A.M., Till, G. (eds), 'British Naval Documents, 1204-1960', *Navy Records Society*, CXXXI (1993).

Ireland, S., *Picturesque views on the river Medway* (1793).

Kelly's Directory of Kent (1862-1937).

Lacy, M., *The female shipwright* (2008 edn, first published 1773).

Lambarde, W., *A perambulation of Kent* (reprinted Bath, 1970, first published 1596).

Latham, R. (ed.), *The Illustrated Pepys* (1978).

Lewis, S., *A Topographical Dictionary of England* (1848).

Mercurius Publicus (24-31 May 1660).

Mercurius Rusticus (1643).

Mitchell, C. (ed.), *Hogarth's peregrination* (Oxford, 1962).

Munro, A., and Row, P., *Rochester and Chatham with their surroundings, a handbook for visitors and residents* (Rochester, 1905).

Oppenheim, M. (ed.), 'The Naval Tracts of Sir William Monson', *Navy Records Society*, Vol. XLVII (1914).

Parfect, C., *Proposals made in the year 1720, to the Parishioners of Strood in Kent for building a Workhouse there … By the Minister of Strood* (London, 1725).

Phillips Bevan, G., *Handbook to the County of Kent* (1876).

Phippen, J., *Description and sketches of Rochester and district* (1862).

Plomer, H., 'The Churchwarden's accounts for St Nicholas at Strood, Part 1, 1555-1600', *Kent Archaeological Society Record Series*, Vol. V (1927).

Powell, J.R. and Timmings, E.K. (eds), 'Documents relating to the Civil War 1642-1648', *Navy Records Society*, Vol. CV (1963).

Saville, A. (ed.), *Secret Comment, the diaries of Gertrude Savile 1721-1757* (Nottingham, 1997).

Seymour, C., *A new Topographical, Historical and Commercial Survey of the Cities, Towns and Villages of the County of Kent* (Canterbury, 1776).

Tombleson, W., *Tombleson's views of the Thames and Medway* (1833-4).

Wrights Topography of Rochester, Chatham, and Strood (Rochester, 1838).

Wylie, W.L. and M.A., *London to the Nore painted and described* (1905).

Newspapers

Some are searchable online on the British Library's 'British Newspapers 1800-1900' website, which can be accessed in some libraries. Others are available on microfilm at the Medway Archives and Local Studies Centre, or at the Centre for Kentish Studies.

Chatham News
Chatham and Rochester News
Chatham Observer
Illustrated Times
Kentish Gazette
Kentish Post
Maidstone Gazette
Rochester and Chatham Journal
Rochester Gazette
Rochester, Chatham & Strood Gazette
The Times

MAPS

One of the earliest maps of the area is the late 16th-century map of *The course of the Medway, from Rochester to the Thames* (BL Cotton Augustus, I.I.52) which offers an indication of the relative size of the four settlements before the dockyards were established. The four Medway Towns are shown in some detail on the Andrews, Drury and Herbert Map of Kent (1769), drawn at a scale of two inches to the mile. Also useful are the maps produced for Edward Hasted's *The History and Topographical Survey of the County of Kent* (1778-90), which also show the principal residences in the area as mentioned in the text. The development of the Medway area and the growth of the urban conurbation can be tracked on the OS 1:50,000 series maps of 1819, 1896 and 1931. Also available is the 1866 OS 1:2500 and the 1:500 series, offering greater detail. These and other local maps can be viewed at Medway Archives and Local Studies Centre.

UNPUBLISHED COLLECTIONS

The following list of record repositories includes a brief note of the main categories of records consulted for this project. This is not an exhaustive list of their respective holdings. After the name of each, the abbreviation used in the endnotes appears in brackets. More information about the repositories and their holdings can be obtained from the related websites.

British Library, London (BL)
Maps, engravings and other images.
www.bl.uk/

Centre for Kentish Studies, Maidstone (CKS)
Wills and probate inventories from Archdeaconry of Rochester court records and from the Deanery of Shoreham; quarter sessions records; family papers and diaries; local newspapers; local history books and journals.
http://www.kent.gov.uk/leisure_and_culture/archives_and_local_history.aspx

Medway Archives and Local Studies Centre, Strood (MALSC)
Parish registers and other parish records; nonconformist records; census; manorial records; local government records; apprenticeship registers; port records, turnpike, charity and poor law records; family and business papers; maps; archive images and photographs; local history books and periodicals.
http://cityark.medway.gov.uk/

The National Archives, Kew (TNA)
Records of the Admiralty and of the Auditors of the Imprest relating to the Medway area; wills and probate inventories.
http://www.nationalarchives.gov.uk/

Staffordshire Archives (SA)
Sutherland papers relating to Sir John Leveson of Halling, Lord Lieutenant of Kent (documents relating to Kent are available on Microfilm at CKS).
http://www.staffordshire.gov.uk/leisure/archives/

ONLINE RESOURCES

http://explore.englandspastforeveryone.org.uk/
The Victoria County History Explore website offers access to a wide range of historical and educational material from EPE projects across the country, including the Medway Valley and Medway Towns Projects in Kent. Materials relating to these projects include transcriptions of wills and probate inventories, census data and images.

http://www.nationalarchives.gov.uk/a2a/
A2A Access to Archives provides a searchable national database of archival material.

www.british-history.ac.uk/
British History Online gives online access to Victoria County History of Kent, Vol. II, and Hasted's *History and Topographical Survey*, and offers a search engine giving access to relevant material contained in other publications on the site.

www.kentarchaeology.org.uk/
This is the website of the Kent Archaeological Society, the county's historical society, offering details of their activities and publications, including their journal *Archaeologica Cantiana*. Also linked to www.kentarchaeology.ac/, the online publishing site of the society.

www.visionofbritain.org.uk/
Vision of Britain provides information on places in Great Britain between 1801 and 2001, including maps, statistical trends and historical descriptions.

Index

Page numbers in *italics* refer to pictures or their captions.

Picture Credits

The authors and publishers wish to thank the following for permission to reproduce their material. Any infringement of copyright is entirely accidental: every care has been taken to contact or trace all copyright owners. We would be pleased to correct in future editions any errors or omissions brought to our attention. References are to page numbers except where stated.

British Library, 4, 24, 27 (Fig. 25), 73

Centre for Kentish Studies, Kent Archives and Local History Service, Kent County Council, 2

English Heritage, 12, 48 (Fig. 38)

Geograph © Danny Robinson, 87, 88 (Fig. 67)

Government Art Collection, 86

Images of England © David G Smith, 95 (Fig. 74)

John Hills © Canterbury Christ Church University, xii, 5, 7 (Fig. 5), 80, 89

Mary Evans Picture Library, 122, 123, 127

Medway Archives and Local Studies Centre, 7 (Fig. 6), 36, 38 (Fig. 30), 41, 74 (Fig. 58), 93, 95 (Fig. 75), 96, 102, 106 (Fig. 80), 109, 115 (Fig. 83), 125 (Figs A and B), 126, 140 (Figs 100 and 101)

Medway Archives and Local Studies Centre, Couchman Collection, 8 (Fig. 7), 15, 48 (Fig. 37), 49, 50, 56 (left), 65, 66 (Fig. 52), 76, 77 (Fig. A), 85, 88 (Fig. 66), 103, 106 (Fig. 81), 108, 115 (Fig. 84), 117, 118 (Figs 86 and 87), 119, 134, 137, 138 (Figs 97 and 98), 139

Nashford Publishing , 13

National Maritime Museum, 17, 18 (Fig. 16), 19, 21 (Figs 19 and 20), 38 (Fig. 29), 44, 47, 58, 61, 66 (Fig. 51), 69, 77 (Fig. B)

National Portrait Gallery, 8 (Fig. 8), 23, 68 (Fig. B), 98

The Pepys Library, Magdalene College, Cambridge, 20

Peter Higginbotham www.workhouses.org.uk, 82

Rijksmuseum, 33, 46

Royal Engineers Museum, 97

Sir John Hawkins Hospital, 68 (Fig. A)

Alex Turner, 130

University of London, 9 (Figs 9 and 10), 10, 18 (Fig. 17), 22, 26, 27 (Fig. 26), 39, 40, 54 (Figs 41 and 42), 55, 56 (right), 57 (Figs 45 and 46), 59, 67 (Figs 53 and 54), 70, 74 (Fig. 59), 90, 92 (Figs 70 and 71), 94, 104, 110, 132